Life in My Eyes

KIONTAE PETTIS

authorHOUSE®

AuthorHouse™
1663 Liberty Drive
Bloomington, IN 47403
www.authorhouse.com
Phone: 1 (800) 839-8640

Published by AuthorHouse 03/11/2016

ISBN: 978-1-5049-6092-2 (sc)
ISBN: 978-1-5049-6091-5 (e)

Library of Congress Control Number: 2015918607

Print information available on the last page.

Letter of Acknowledgment

I would like to thank my team AuthorHouse for all of their hard work and effectors upon my work. I appreciate the chance you have taken upon me as an author, I would like to especially thank Mae Genson, Rhae Nolan, Joseph Elan, and Francine Diola. I couldn't make this book a success without you all I welcome you to life in my eyes!

Epilog I Am God

I am the sun which provides life. I am God which provides Christ, I am the words of the wise listen to my advice, I shine even in the dark I am light. I am respect I am polite, spiritually I cut deep I am a knife. I am out of this world an unreachable height. I am a man I must fight, I am a nuke upon evil ready to ignite! I am a plane forever on a flight, I am unseen by a naked eye simply out of site. I am the day and the night, I am strike full I do bite, I am the moon which shines bright, I am the opposite of unplanned simply out of spite. I am success I am fame heading to go far, I am a star unreachable by a car. I am the people I know who we are! I am the wind shall I blow, I am the spirit hidden inside concealing every soul. I am the one that shall come if you die before you wake, I listen and grant covenant deeds. I am the reason you pray, I am the reason the blessings to Earth you receive. I am in your veins when you bleed. I am karma, may react upon humanity fast or slow. I am not a human forever an angle. The clock of existence, for when it is time I will call. I am the one that catches those who fall, I am the one who created the commandments, more important than laws. I am the giving tree standing tall, providing air to bare to you all. I am the hurricanes, tornadoes, earthquakes, tsunamis, and every other destructive things I am Mother Nature son, I am fate soon to come win or lose, to this Earth I am the fuse. I am heaven's gate not to accept everyone, I am the solar system and galaxies, I provide peace seized on our spirituality. I am the end the last fatality, I am the king all shall praise to me. I am God and judgment day you will see!

Prolog: My story

I know God who you are, I hope you're not far in a galaxy. Don't let the Devil take over my spirituality, all he seeks is revenge and fatality. I'm with you lord don't doubt me. I was an accident baby, so many tears in my eyes drove my daddy crazy and my momma left me did me shady. Praying every day to the lord lately hoping that there's room for me on the other side? Together we will rise like the sunshine for every sin and lie I've committed I apologize. The Devil had me hypnotized, but I had to get away and strategize. We are all made equal you and me! All God's clan for every women and man, it was God's plan how it all begin. He died on the cross for all our sins to awakening Christ and live an eternal life, in the end, I feel like all I ever been is cursed. Just ask the nurse momma did me the worst. For all, it's worth I forgave but haven't forgotten because the pain isn't stopping. Dear God tell what am I'm here for? Was it implied for me to be born? Every day is a blessing, I use my mind as a weapon to bring change, but still I remain insane trying to stay in my own lane higher than you all auto piolet on my own plane. They say you can use only 20% of the brain but when I rhyme I obtain the full thing. I was never perfect steady cautious and nervous because I find a lot isn't worth it. I hear people telling me how they committed felonies, and when you black there is racism and jealousy. I thought the word was full of magical creatures and peace, then it seized to me there's barely any open opportunities. People dying in our communities! There's no being safe, no promised tomorrow fate, girls constantly getting raped, and the world just full of hate! I had thoughts to gravitate and escalate my name, I'm a nobody but to God I'm somebody, and I feel I'm equal like everybody, but everything isn't what it seems. So many drugs out there turning people to Fein's. The Devil try's to grasp me, I scream! I close my eyes and the light of God beams at me! God telling me "us together is the only strategy" to build my fate and make a space in those lines through Heaven's gate. Walk by faith not by sight something I try and might, but without seeing how can I stand to fight? See if everything's alright! I then feel blind depression strikes. I'm stressed and there's so little time. That's when I take a pen and write rhymes lines after lines that defines, thoughts flowing out my mind. I know I got to hustle, grind, shine, and climb over those mountains. Believe and show no doubting, I can't feel at ease if I'm not where the Church be. The Devil never shows any mercy. Every time I pray to God, I wait but haven't heard him speak. I hope with my spirit through praying to him I even reach, and the Devil doesn't win I sin and began a road to go underneath. I'm only human, so of course at times by the Devil I'm reached. I was always too scared to die, but still the conscience of my mind telling me suicide! I looked in the mirror and stared and thought to myself who am I? I don't know me, I don't hold many good memories. I'm not broken, but left empty, left unsolved, that isn't all I can't fall, but I know the lord will one day call, will I be ready for my time here to end? Will I go to Heaven, and see all my family, and all my friends. It feels immaculate, I wasn't planned I was an accident! Never knew what she was made of. Who could I trust then? I don't believe in love! I don't believe in a second chance, or a mistake, but regret that my past is my past, it went by too fast to fix, and it's too late! My mind shakes and earthquakes, I work out but my soul is not in a better shape. I got many dreams and talents, I want to be this, I want to do that, but when the time comes and my future isn't fun, my dreams crumble it begins it runs, how will I react? Will I turn back delete, subtract, or tell myself, I 'ma get it if any means build my team, chase my dreams, and accomplish everything. I remember when I was 7, I used to draw had skills and an incredible imagination, but how could have suffered? I never experienced segregation, jail, bail, probation, or committed a crime. I find, that I can't even grasp my mind. Everything is going by so fast I'm losing time, to complete everything, every dream, and show the world me. I have faith and do believe, that I won't just be left to bury in a cemetery and let the rest be history. I hope it isn't too late we learn from our mistakes. I haven't experienced amusement allusions, this is my story my hand written rhyming constitution. Each rhyme provides the substitution for me to go up inflation. I wish I really felt to myself only God can judge me. I wish I could go back and hope I don't OD on CD tracks, and it's a fact that being black can be worse than being fat or o-beast, constantly terrorized by the police, putting handcuffs on G's, "Telling them you don't have the right to speak" Man everything happens for a reasons, there's a few seasons, and reasons for weather changes. When it's hot I hope to shine. When it rains, I hope it reimburse the thirst written in my lines, if it snows I'll know I'm cold, and got to change my flows, when the sun rose I was shining I glowed, and God let know, if not let me go. I'm losing control, stuck in a final stage of complete man rage. I open the book, but haven't got past the first page, first grade, you haven't spoken to me verbally. Please give me hope and clues like charades, don't let me fade, and let the Devil degrade. Have room for me in those gates. Show us why we are blessed, to be in this world and stay. My road, ancient times, and glory. My life my journey my story!

1. Do you feel what I feel: I'm 21 feeling younger and lost in this world? Cherishing my family, but cannot trust a girl. Now and why have I realized that things have turned so different for you and me? Can't even grasp who I am and what I want to be. Feel like my soul is trapped in a cell in jail, but this isn't not monopoly. Only I can stop me from success and to succeed things I feel I will achieve and need. In the end, what will I really receive? Life is a blessing a long journey and lesson. A lot of things we do we question? We try to make our investments, and maintain it. A lot of people fake it, me I'm trying to chase it, and these bad memories that be killing me I wish I could erase it. Instead, I use them to advantage. Which lets me know what's real because life's so hard to manage. Troubles on top of troubles, it all doubles, and when we grasp that chance to it all, that ball sometimes we fumble. Fight for our beliefs, like a rumble. Something tells me I shall be famous, not hated speculated and mistaken, but strive for success this life is a test, like preparation. God shall be our motivation, Glad we over the bad the mad the slaves, and segregation. The depth has rained life will never be the same. Robbery and poverty, it seems this gracious world of ours is coming to an end, or people just committing sins. Some follow below where the demons are. Which will you choose to rot in a cell, succeed or fail, make it out of jail, barely can afford bail, yeah we all got regrets, all make bets, try to show off get into contests, These bullets are eating our flesh, has caused so many deaths, Life taken over anger, has put so many in danger. So much confusion, school shootings, people suffering abused, and the people committing it all for amusement. What the hell is wrong with the world today? Can't even walk outside cross the street freeway or interstate. People shot dying, and it isn't even their fate. That's why I hope and pray every day we stay in God's hands. Where we shall be safe, where there's no hate, no race, living in sanctuary, every single day. Which will you choose Heaven or Hell Succeed or fall? Only time will tell, but do you feel what I feel?

2. Days of being blind: For eternity I will search for a sign, time after time I hope fate doesn't recline. For I'm weary in Days of being blind, not seeing outside my soul. Not seeing how ball would roll and penetrate a goal. Seeing how could I control? Accept no defeat salvation shall retreat. Wars of before cold wars, world wars, all over land, freedom, religion, and race. It's the world we're place, it seems the cause and effect of what we face history has given a trace. What of a naked eye, what of a blind man's pride? It seems the nation to humanity can hide. It isn't political, as a man with his mistress bride. Land of trail, lavish grail, the world auctions we the "puppets" all for sale. Held on due to fame popularity it's, all the same, selling their soul, selling their fate. May they counter plate the wrong slate, the wrong vanity, morally wrong traits? If all were true to real facts, how would one react? How can another be exact? It seems the one who knows the truth, the secret among society attacks. It's hidden like the message on a dime. I pray in due time humanity reclines, days of being blind!

3. Stay committed to you: Roses are red, violets are blue. I was mistaken for a lie, but I spoke the truth. Soon as I looked into your eyes, I felt my feelings run loose. She said "she's not looking for a man" so I'm not the one to choose, but I came in as a friend so I got closer to you. Feeling nervous inside I don't know what to say or do, but I let the moment play and kept my cool. Kind of easy of holding a conversation, when I speaking with you. Real easy to lie, but hard to tell the truth. I just took a break, went into a huddle. Got lost with the play, now I'm stuck in a huddle. Was because I didn't give it my all, and my feelings turn subtle? then I feared competition so I feared a little trouble, but I came back in the game and made it all double. I just hate the word relationship, but I been searching in time with a spaceship. I don't have time to be tied down, and feeling whipped, because too many come and go like a dealership so I 'ma stay committed to you like it was in the begging. When I felt to myself I was most winning. Roses are red, violets are blue, I felt the connection turn real, so I' ma stay committed to you.

4. Valentines, valentines: Valentine's, Valentine's kind of slips my mind because love is left behind. So I set out to search and find, but not today on Valentine's. Chocolates, roses, and love are what it's all made of. Happy connecting love and affection, to your selection. That one Valentine you have, did you feel that day perfecting? Holding each other and kissing some want that for this day there fishing. People wait every year for this day, looking back and forward seeing if love changed that person you love those feelings inside can't explain. You look at their eyes and your heart beats but you're not traumatized the love before you, you realized body languages doesn't lie. It's just you and her all in your own world it's more than straight it curls. Those gifts necklets diamonds roses and pearls can have so much affection on a girl. Money certain presents for a guy, whatever you get shows you tried. Valentine's, Valentine's a different time connecting with different signs Valentine's, Valentine's.

5. Dear lord: Dear lord I hope these words to you, reach. I know I don't know the true meaning of life, so please teach me. When I die please Lord don't let me go underneath, because at any time the Devil is trying to creep when I fall please sweep me off my feet. I'm so thankful for right now, and to be able to wake out my sleep. I'm thankful for breakfast, or every time I eat. Dear lord open those close doors. Make a life a thing for me to explore make a list you want me to do like chores. Please, Lord, don't let me fall weak. When I pray to you, God I just want to hear you speak. I want to follow your plan every day of the week. Lord it's so hard to let go of my old ways, sinning, and take your name in vain. Please let me rise above it I know when you brought me to this world, I was supposed to be something. At times it gets hard when I pray to you, take me in your world like mars. Let me shine God like one of those stars. I can feel you close I'm just hoping you're not far. Just tell me what to do, and every possible way to get closer to you. Yes indeed, get me past greed, let me succeed and achieve what I need. Don't rest on me, the Devil is cruelty most absolutely. Please, lord, see through me flip through my heart like a T.V. Keep me away from enemies, yes I know you feel me? What did you think last time I prayed recently? So to the power invested in me, what would your plans be for me? Please open more opportunities. You are the only I apprehend, Lord forgive me for my sins. At the end of it all let me make it through them gates, where you are and next to my family.

6. The eye of a guy: See, every man that are addicted to women, rather its sex their image the way they are appealing. There's a lot of girls multiple over a million. Different types from blacks, Mexicans, and whites. I'm trying to see how these girls sprout. From the early ages faces, and temptations of being a Girl Scout love they can't do without. It's a cold world for these girls. So I set out for a girl, to support her they come and go there's no order. It's kind of funny how good things don't last forever. Things slip out in the rain when that sunshine's I can feel their pain. The clouds are soft, like if I were to lay on you and left my mind dissolve tempted to see you take it off. I'm not the type to ask for much I know couples argue and fuss. Nobody's conversation is perfect, but with God say to you. It's like I am the one to pray day by day, making sure that girls out there are safe and another won't take hoping she doesn't escape. Guys be wondering why she with him? Why she with her? Maybe because it's about that deeper feeling running inside your veins. Those chemicals sent to your brain those feelings can't obtain. Don't judge a cover by its book, those pages what lies in inside tell a guy why she's shy, and why she just can't trust a guy. She's thinking he is investing for sex, and if she let, would it just be a booty call or a bet. Will she be worth the time kept, or cheated on used and left? Will you take that journey study her everything, background, and heritage. Ask her in the future for marriage? We all got chances after chances for romances. In the end of it all which women is going to be your soul mate at the end of your fate? We as guys need to have a clue. Women are worth so much more to explore. It isn't easy to earn a key to her lock door, and when you do get a chance take it step by step, moment by

3

moment, day by day, and thank God every day for these beautiful women he creates!

7. Together we're fine: Together we fine: Love is pain, pain is pleasure her skin soft as feathers. Makeup on the mirror on the dresser, catches her reflection. She's a 10 a perfect complexion, must be from a different dimension. I search for her with my telescope she embraces the attention. So many girls out there more than a million, but she different gifted morally optimistic. She's clean beauty sticks out in the scene, but there's no I in team. It's like I see her but can't obtain. She's driving next me but in the other lane. Guess I got to catch a flight on a plane, light a torch to her heart because her body language doesn't explain. You are the one I prospect, and with you, I want to connect. So open up then I might fetch. Your heart might drop but trust I' ma catch, like if u were dead in my bed u I would resurrect. Rubbing on your flesh kissing on your neck. Not trying to rush, but its lush if I don't know if I'm enough, or worth it God's gift so you're perfect. I' ma pray for you in advance cause your worth it. No circus or clown when it's all said and done and the run is fun you are the one with the crown. Build my community with you a town. No birthday but you're sweeter than cake, wear my love as a cape. Each step you take just know in my gates you're safe. Burger king have it your way. On that wedding day, let us cherish and inherit I'll commit my values to you I ain't embarrassed. Just loving the opportunity, I'm trying to make this clear it's better you and me. I 'ma stay in line like your spine, whatever it is you want I can't decline. We got our own love watch, so cherish the time. As long as God on our side, together we're fine!

8. Days of riding behind a trash truck: Monday through Friday is scheduled up for me, days of riding behind a trash along truck. At 5:30 am I wake up brush my teeth I go to work clock in then ride in the company truck to my route. Once we arrived to the route I get out and start behind on the trash truck hanging on the back of the truck. Towards the back of the truck is two steps for me and my helper we hold on the bars on the side of the truck. We get off house to house throwing trash bags, tables, chairs, couches, tree branches cut up to 6 feet and up to 50 pounds of weight but some things weight more. The job has got me in the best of shape seems my endurance has put on a cape. I work for republic services the days are all the same all a repeat, I wake up brush my teeth eat and clock in by 6:30 am. I leave the job by 6:45 am and start trash on my route about 7:10 am. Throughout the whole day we get two loads or more up to 12 tons a load. Now it's getting very cold I have been working here since 18 years old next February I'll be 22 years old. As a trash man I have worked in the most serious conditions working in 100-degree weather of the summer the heat of the sun overwhelming me. Working in the cold running to keep myself warm I fear nothing the trash won't harm. The art of riding on a trash truck is a different view seeing ranches, nice, homes, gated, communities, animals, and insects. Republic services is a multi-million dollar company who takes safety seriously and values their employees. I have gotten into an accident once in my career. I was picking up glass in the summertime and I sat the glass on the compacter to throw it in the packer in the back of the truck where the trash gets compacted the glass shattered on me. It cut my right forearm, I got cut to the muscle they took me to the clinic and I had gotten 4 stitches in my muscle 20 staples across my arm. I had lost all my strength, I was going to therapy to work on rebuilding my strength in my right arm. I did exercises with my arm I worked on rehabilitating my muscle by shaping my right hand with sign language and using objects to gain muscle memory in shaping and forming. I was in a lot of pain I was so weak at a point I had did a squeeze test on strength my left and right arm. My left arm squeezed 65 pounds of pressure my right arm only squeezed 10 pounds. I had to get my strength back I was on light duty at my job helping with whatever I could. I was off work for about two months. I overcame this chapter of my life and I got my full strength back my stadium and endurance. This was my fault for not asking for help and improperly throwing the glass away. I am left with a really bad scar now but I thankful to be alive I have had some good times with my company. I learn that if we fall down we can get back up I learn I can overcome anything, days of riding on the back of a trash.

9. To be a man: To become a "man" takes pride. To be a man you must understand it's more than a job, more than a person more than a figure of speech. As a man, we have several goals to reach, several responsibilities and the capability of completing almost anything. A man takes prior steps to maintain self-esteem, and self-respect good luck shall be kept. You take experiences of life what's fake and what's left. To begin strive to be your best. You dream of ways to reach success. As a man, we must grow take your time take things slow. Being a man is something we don't know, as a person your image shows. You are able to control your life. As the journey goes on you learn your wrongs from rights. If something is important to you, you will fight it's the way of life. From a child, boy to a man, with the bible on your side in your hands. You have the key to being a man!

10. By the sunrise: The sun rose this morning, but I was lonely like today this moment. Only God has a plan and a girl for me that he is condoning. So I let my heart and these moments play. The sun and its waves I can't escape. Day by day, I pray for that special girl to appear and come my way. So far I haven't had much of a clue, or realized but I hope we meet at the sunrise. Let the flowers bloom, and let there be a sweet smell that I can tell it's her perfume. When that day comes by, let me stare into her eyes and her beauty is like the sunrise. When the sun comes down and there's no sunlight, let her be my sunlight. I search in the solar system, looking through the planets and stars. I hope she's not too far! By God bring her to me. When the sun is almost down, when that sunrise comes and with her I will no longer frown. We will lay on the clouds, and with her, I will lay on the clouds looking down seeing who's passing by. Let her come by the sunrise.

11. Mad: Being Mad is a feeling that when reached, it begins a stage of rage. Your moment fades, madness stays, and you're in a daze. The fire burns in your veins all you think is about is pain. You ball your fist, grin your teeth, your feelings twist, you begin pissed, and you're feeling in abyss, your only wish is to show that person what they're truly dealing with. The anger can put others in danger from a woman to a man to any stranger. Mad is the opposite of sad, it can turn a conversation bad a feeling we wish we couldn't have and grasp. You become discombobulated, separated, and those who have put you at this stage for reasons you start hating. The concentration of letting it all go when you're mad your whole image will show. The feeling comes and goes you lose control. It's not always your bad, we are all humans throughout life we get mad.

12. Beauty: Beauty is more than a look, first off don't judge a cover by its book. I know that image shows so we got to look. Deep inside lies the key so we usually are blind. It's a hallucinating in the mind because true beauty is hard to find. Her personality is compatible with her sign. Overtime is when beauty is reached, not by surgery, rarely being teach, and for a living queen, it seems it's hardly reached. Beauty is defined differently for me because we all got our own taste. Some have beauty but put makeup on it may be fake. Those seem cute might not relate. Some stuck up and hard to conversate with. She's tired of a man looking to get into her pants. Her plan is to find the right man for romance in the future get on his knees pull out the ring in his hands and say marry me. Your decision reflects your destiny. How you dress to impress and show your self-respect is the key. Beauty gets stripped and it isn't they fault. The ones that are dimes, guys searching to find them there thirsty they stalk. It's more than makeup we search for what you are made of. The truth comes out when you wake up because every girl isn't what they seem. Some girls addicted to sex and turn out to be feigns. Every girl has a freaky side, once they decide they are down to ride. They turn out to invest in more guys that's when sex is kept, and the weakness multiplies. That's not always for the better because that body you have doesn't last forever. Shout out to them models, hotties, dimes, and cuties, you all represent the definition of beauty. Many girls are to attention cash diamonds and pearls but in all truth, there's beauty that lies in every girl.

13. Females and girls: Why is my selection based on a girl's complexion? Shall I show she's worth my full affection? These girls complexion some judge by they looks, style, smile, and ass. The one's bad either cocky or fast did some things in the past. Those memories lie in their hearts and forever last. Forward and back they roam the streets. Women addicted to sex that feeling which can make them weak. Some are strippers independent workers on they own, and some many hurt her, dessert her, used her time, she's fine, but she find that these dudes feeling choose used her for amusement and abused. When is man gone get it together? Treat that one like they treasure. That one gift stop calling females words like a hoe, slut, and bitch. You see we need to search on what's on the inside, not the out. Look into her mind see if she sprouts. Figure out her doubts what she all about? Does her personality match will your love for her hatch? Will she be like a dollar lotto ticket used and scratch, thrown on the ground, or will you pray to God if she truly the one you need and found? Will she be your queen in the end when she smiles your heart drops? So many out there multiple shots. Each relationship helps the next these girls are like a test. Some hard as hell and need studying. Some are easy A and addicted to playing like things your way. It doesn't take a day, to find your soul mate that God made!

14.   Searching out for her: I'm searching out for you baby, looking through the clouds and mountains. Your love, the only thing I'm accounting. I want to drink from your fountain or else I'm drowning. Waiting for that special day on my calendar counting. Searching for the one, I glared at the sunrise waiting for you to come up like the sun. The one I can pick up in my heart for the run. I see them mistakes it's too late. So I'm sitting sleep dreaming in my head waiting for my dream to come true. I'm chasing after you but don't know what to do, but follow each footprint which leads right to you. She's staring at me "I'm like damn is it true" My heart starts to beat feeling too good to be true so I'm weak because you creeping all on me I found the one most certainly. Mirror on the crystal bowl shows the future and all. I see your face on the ball, so tell me my future to come? Will I glare at her eyes and her height is like the sun? Will she give into me let the moment play run, or take my hand I'll be your man understand all I am is fun. Sleeping in my palace when you wake up promise you'll be smiling. Well asleep when the day is the done, but we just begun. She open the door trying to see what's in stored. Each steps what's next take it slow. Please let me control, let it all show. You give into me I give it all to you, I call it give and go. So relax kick back put your shoes on the mat. Walking through paradise, there's no turning back. Chief cooking dinner anything you need just ask for that. Hair did makeup did super fine on some dime shit. She naked in my bed massaging my back while I'm holding and kissing her hand. I know you understand let us expand. Getting you in a white dress saying yes is the plan. So let me paint a picture of your sculpture, body so amazing. Feeling on your body nobody going to give you this closer. So let's start for your heart cupid love baby never fall apart. Sex, love, passion, high effects with attractions. Let's make a run play I'll be your Reggie bush, you're my Kim Kardashian. Neckless, bracelets, earwigs, luxury with those heels. Baby dress to impress and I'm feeling your appeal. You the deal, baby be killing me body smoother than a symphony. Cinderella love nothing above baby you're my recipe stay to the death of me. Tiger woods swing take you out of this world on a new planted. With me a family tree, like seeds how many would we have planted? Promise to be there when you pregnant. When your stomach big, I'm not embarrassed. Love rain on me like it's lighting when you kiss me got my heart igniting. Kissing on your neck equals love no stress baby this forever and I swear you the best. You're my queen I'm your king this is our life like chest.

15. Till death do us apart: I knew you had my heart from the start, but I was blind to the big picture God's destiny and work of art. Then suddenly cupid shot his dart. You shined in the light brighter than the sun. I waited by the sunrise for you to come special not just anyone. It began fun as the sun went away you faded away. When the dark sparked at the end of the day God perpetually took you away. I sat waiting and prayed, there I stood there I sat there I laid. Couldn't eat couldn't sleep mourn weeping it cut me so deep. You were my other half only together as one I'll be complete. Only then I will no longer fantasize in my dreams but actually sleep. I climbed closer to you up to the mountains peak. When the sun rose it was so unique. Though I felt so much heat that couldn't stop me. I can't resist my chance I can't miss me and u together forever I wish. When the sun smiles you blow me a kiss without lips just a face now no body no hips but the right time I must predict. I sailed to the west but left my soul in the east. You are true beauty I am the beast nevertheless its critique I walk in no shoes bleeding of misery pain targets my feet. Then one day the bird passed me by I caught it with my 3rd eye it took me to fly by surprise then finally, we met you and me. I can't lie the light is much more loving than the dark, the shadow of you follows me till death do us apart!

16. My mind: My mind is uncertain, I think about a lot I have this big imagination to fully express myself I speak to me hardly anybody else. My mind seems crazy no memories as a baby Just writing poetry lately. I try to dissect my brain the thoughts that come across and what's left. I close my eyes take a breath my brain sends a signal to take a step. When I'm tired my mind's thinking rest but I don't want to till I fully shut down my mind is full of dreams but I'm constantly let down. My mind is crazy I can't play around. I analyze and watch others make very little sounds. For exchange ignore my heart and use my brains because they don't both feel the same. A mind is a terrible thing to waste I can smell, see, and taste, but when I stand face to face my mind wanders away. I don't ignore signs I read between lines, but I find everything is my mind.

17. Dear bro: I want to take this time, to dedicate this to my brother that's mine. RIP Detra Demetrius Howard. Dear bro, I hope you know that I still think about you. At times, I put myself in your shoes and think what would he do? I know you in eaven and been disappeared. I feel your spirit close so you still here. I know you looking down you smile in your heart but watching makes you frown. It's crazy I never realize that was the end for you and I. Tears in my eyes hate multiply as soon as you died. I will never forget matter fact I admit. You pointed out my flaws and the stupid things I did you tried to fix. I watch who you were around and with the love you had kept in my heart left equipped. Damn it's crazy how I hope I reach out to you with rhymes it's 5/29(15) and I finally decided to write to you and it took time, well over the last year I reminisce that you not here. Man, it hurts so bad just thinking how you died makes me cry and feel so mad because I know when you was coming up you didn't see much of your dad. You were a momma's boy probably was her favorite like a boy's favorite toy. When u were around filled her heart with joy, how do I feel right now? Kind of down at this moment my heart writes and my mind makes no sound. I miss those days when u was around. They were most fun we used to play the video to let the time run. Who would have thought you get killed by a gun? That's when everything fell apart. Momma scared because a peace had left of her heart. The reason why I hadn't said much is because it hurts so much to discuss. When the person you love helped you be a man and come up. We used to chill from night to the sun up looking back got my mind messed up. I don't know what to do should I pray and wait for my time to be right next to you? You started a family just had twins but they killed you hurt the whole family took you out the crew. It isn't like a screw I can't get a screwdriver and put the nail back in the killer was probably your friend. Now it begins for the life of your twins it's messed up not knowing they dad or what they had. Each birthday your son got the same day probably makes him cry and mad if he blew out the candles for a wish probably want his dad. It isn't serious till you lose what you have. Times we spent together I swear to God makes me glad. I just want you to know I cherish every memory we had and reminisce on every single bad. This is so touchy I can't let it go. Why you have to die was it the Devil? People jealous cause u was a handful now you with God on another level. At your funeral a handful of tears were flowing through my eyes and I couldn't hold them in. No one can relate to you like I can, not even your friends would ride by your side like I until the end. Every day I wake up I think about my bro it sucks forever I know I got to let it go. I know you're doing better I'm sorry for all my lies I apologize, bro, now I'm traumatized. I dedicate this to a girl who has love for you over any girl your love lost in this world, her name is Deondra, your Baby mama. She's more hurt than anyone probably even momma. Memories in my heart but I'm left empty now you gone your flesh left in the cemetery. Now Deondra left for your kids to carry. It hurts my heart so much when you was buried. I guess God I'll let it go I never will forget our times you got killed by the men by the Devil. Well, you sprouted through life like a flower. Detra Demetrius

Howard had power and never was a coward. I apologize lord let him recognize! Well goodbye I got to let it go, Rip (rest in peace) bro.

18. Life: Life is precious my presence is a living blessing. Day by day life goes on and things fly by. We all one day must die. We cry, we sin, lie, apologize, and recognize that life is different for a girl and guy. Life is a test we suffer, stress, and at times things are a mess. To overcome those challenges takes patience, faith, and belief that throughout life we can achieve and overcome almost anything. Life is not a game you have a name and you grow up experiencing everyone is not the same. We don't know exactly why we are here but a lot take life for granted they don't care. Throughout the times you shared just know God, is watching was there he cares. We all are made equal not to compare, but reality it's all different full of pure competition. We grow through life changing stepping stones from being a baby, young grown too old we don't realize that life is gold. It's more than you can grasp from the good times the bad the sad and mad through all the times you had. We still don't know how good the life you have. We all are planted seeds from a long existing family tree trying to be what they want to be. Some don't get what they want it's only a plan of the Lord the spirit of God is more than we can afford. It's me all pick and seized to believe that life is something we love and need. We stand, fight, sweat, talk, walk, learn earn, accomplish, strive, glide cry, multiply, and die but with God in our spirits we shall be alright. It's our journey and times its life.

19. Hope: When I'm tied against the rope, the only thing that will get me through is hope. Dreams of me to succeed no longer being broke staying in church listening words of the pope. Day by day I got to hope the Lord provides faith. Regulate my ever step and destiny my living prophecy. I hope to God the Devil can't stop thee. The people the sequel the last of a dying breed and multiple planted seeds. Yes, indeed I hope to achieve my dreams and fantasies because life isn't what it seems and planned to be. I feel the spirit of the Holy Ghost in me controlling the most but what will I do when I'm stuck against the rope? I pray to God to overcome and float with his faith every day I see hope!

20. Time: The time of life ticks and stops. As we sit and watch the time does not stop 24 hours in a day, 31 days in most months 12 months in a year 4 seasons in a year. I fear that time will be ending I feel it near soon we will all disappear and all of the journeys will end here. You see people don't understand the meaning of time: testament, immanent, motive, esteem in time we find the future and the past left behind. Time is priceless something we can't buy but realize that we all are born and eventually will die. It's regulating you and me time.

21. Searching: I don't know why I am here? I search for answers they seem to disappear, have no fear I search for what's near. Maybe the real me maybe a girl searching for why we are all placed in this world? I ask God a lot hoping the blessings he has brought the answers will be caught. Shall I pray and wait still searching every day for who I am and what will come into me forming as a man I want to be the best I can. The plan is for me to be under God's hand because the Devil can suck you in like quicksand. He provokes you to be his friend gives you reasons to lurk, hurt, dessert, and do bad work. When I pray I search for God for, for the truth of everything have no secrets the answers to my deeds I will seek it. I'm born on Earth curious with thirst. Every day I search I wait, watch, and pray my soul is lurking. Every day I'm searching.

22. Am I: Am I guilty of loving a woman with a past? Dear God, I ask when I see through a mirror shall I break the glass. Am I guilty to sin and pretend it's not so bad but try to let go saying never again threading the needle in my skin? Am I selfish because feelings of a woman I don't understand but apprehend? Am I a son of you? Constantly the Devil provokes wrong in my heart look what I been through. Am I clueless for praying every day still I foresight a destiny hoping I see you someday. I wish I were an angle and could fly. If I die would Heaven be my outcry the sequel to my demise. I shall separate my dignity and pride hopefully glide to be welcome for a place met for you and I. Am I already an angel without wings they seem to set aside am I?

23. Colors of the Earth: Evolution evolved through the colors of the earth. The sky is blue trees are green it seems color is everything. Think of creatures, insects, animals, to the eye color is 3d color has a value that can never be detained it works all together like the world we are in. Different colors add up to different colors they fuse together just atoms and all components of life make up the earth. Water is blue just as most of our body is made of trees are green, grass, money, insects are also green bees are yellow ants are black dogs are black, brown, and white. Color is a compound of human nature a way of life people don't know what it's really worth. It's all in God's hand the colors of earth.

24. To achieve you must believe: To achieve you must believe, that you can accomplish anything. Stay consistent and keep chasing you know what you're after to overcome that challenge you're facing your wanting you must be patient, and to achieve you must believe.

25. Weather: Some days it rains then the weather changes different faces of weather for different places. Just a change in the wind then the weather begins some days it will be hot burning still the world's turning. Then it begins to snow you feel chills you're cold. That's when you wear more clothes. The weather is something we cannot control but the weather is not forever days and seasons summer is hot the sun it at its peak. The winter is when it's ice cold in the fall leafs grow the spring is when it rains and snows it gets better. We still live our normal lives in the weather because together we see the weather.

26.   Night: The sun comes down the moonlight begins bright it is night, some of us do fright the precious night. It's dark and without light, we cannot see the moment of time the sun fully leaves. The weather drops it's no longer hot look what the night has brought. Quiet planes in the air on auto piolet people still working crooks lurking, People still being born in the hospital the night is an obstacle. It's when we lay our heads and go to bed stories are heard tucking your children in the bed. It's the opposite of the day and light it's night.

27.   A dream: As you close your eyes and fade away your dream then takes you away. We don't know why we have them and what's in stored. When we dream as we sleep there comes more. Maybe you had a dream that became real maybe you're in that dream and everything feels real. You feel what your dream is doing to you some too good to be true. I had a dream that I will one day see God be in Heaven and he will explain everything to me. Why I am here what I am supposed to do and how I can improve but what will I lose? I dream many dreams and pray let God take you away before you wake. Is it possible that dreams become true? Throughout it, you go with it don't know what to do. Sometimes you seem confused that moment comes when you wake up everything hits you try to go back to that stage but miss you can't resist that. Everyday isn't what it seem you close your eyes and realize you're living an everyday dream. Don't be scared it's only met for you, the images beam you all have seen a dream.

28.   Religions and race: Each human and face consist of religions and race. We all are made by God but hold our own ancestors and family tree. What do you see in this beautiful place? There are many religions and race? Some people have beliefs and rules to follow some live every day the same and routines that follow till tomorrow. We have different skin tones speak different languages born in different places. Overall we are all made by God blessed. We stand strong together forever every day we are the key to religions and race.

29.   Sticks and stones may break my bones but words will never hurt me: Although the world can be ugly don't let words break your nerves. From hurting words you've heard just know words can't hurt you, they can only trip your mood. A lot of people are rude in those situations what should you do? Quick to make a wrongful move but don't let words get to you. Relax take a breath walk away

He's the type who takes initiative.

take a step. Don't worry let's not let things go wrong. Sticks and stones may break your bones uncertainty but words will never hurt me.

30. A happy home: I hate the old times are gone when we were all together in a happy home. Why the hell as things gone wrong? Nothing but arguing and fighting fussing breaking silence to violence. I come home already stressed out knowing that soon they will begin to shout. The bird screams the dog barks it can be daylight or dark. The family just breaking apart how did it all start? It's always something arguing, fighting, and fussing "bitch, hoe, slut'" all for what? Rage, rage, rage can we ever change this page? They're always putting on an act it never dissolves seems like improve. It's, all the same, every single day. Why can't we got to church and pray? All over finances arguing and fighting always fussing breaking silence to violence. Will this madness ever cast away? I'd rather be gone it seems only in Heaven with God there's a happy home.

31. That' what friends are for: A friend a woman or man. A person who will understand and ride for you, in the end, a friend. The person you can talk to about such and such one who doesn't judge. A person that can forgive, give, and adapt to how you live. A companion and partner in life only a friend can tell you what's right. A person you go to for advice someone who's respect and act nice it's a part of life. More than a helping hand, we all have lifelong friends. A woman or man, a friend.

32. An enemy: An enemy is the Devil, a person that would want you buried with a shovel. A hateful person towards you. The enemy wants to destroy you maybe its revenge or just plain hate. Day by day the enemy is wishing that you aren't safe. The enemy can be in your circle close acting as a friend but a foe. How would you know if the enemy doesn't show? When it's an enemy soon you will know. In a lifetime, we will have plenty not just a hater but an enemy.

33. IF I shall die before I wake: If I shall die before I wake I pray I get accepted into Heaven's gate to God my shall spirit fly's away. May I rest in peace no more stress and misery. Let the rest be history, let the answers be solved, let God tell it all, and at the time, he calls I pray and fade away because tomorrow is not a promised day. The Devil seeks my soul to take but I have faith I am saved by God in this place If I shall die before I wake.

34. Karma: Karma is more than a consequence or what's coming back, in fact, karma reacts on the certain bad things you do. No one knows what karma has in stored for you, it can be worse than revenge its God acting that is planned. It can be little can be big but will you reminisce on what you did. Before karma hit's karma's forever doesn't quit. It's something we all have experienced and constantly get. There is good karma and bad never know how long karma will last. The consequence of nature armor is karma.

35. Why am I here: Dear God, why was I born? why am I here? What is my purpose on Earth and who should I fear? When will the Devil disappear? When will I feel your spirit close and near? Am I supposed to bring change to my everyday life that feels the same? I have a name and I am placed in this game. What will I become? A man to start his own family, and you planned out my destiny? What will I do gain and lose? What choices will I make my faith to choose? I am here but what do I prove to you? I know you care this life we all live seems unfair. I ask you, God, why am I here?

36. The road never ends: Through life of all the times we spend, it begins to spin but the road never ends. Not for just us but more to come more journeys begins as the road never ends. More things happen people reactions come out to be satisfaction. What will we do? Where do we go? So many places to explore many sites to adore. From country to states just wait and see where we go, on the road places we see again and again. We must know the road never ends.

37. Separate: When God created this world he had to separate a lot. Heaven where he is kept and where we hope to be brought. Hell, where Satan sees you, to rot. He separate a lot in this life creature from animals the good the bad religions and race each individual changed face. Place from place, some separate people enemy's and evil. Through life, the sequel is for all of us to be equal. We are blessed to be in this special place. Look at how the world runs things will always separate.

38. I abide by his rules: Loyalty, loyal to my family respect all especially the elderly. Laws of nature met for humanity God first please sustain my insanity. Honor thy mother and father responsible for our family tree pray to God daily and faithfully. The 10 commandments created before we assure afterlife is Heaven, our destiny. Sometimes I feel my sins flickering upon my soul. The Devil duels fire lies inside, which is the fuel. Karma can be cruel to life I'm just a mule. I worship God I abide by his rules.

39. Cry: Sometimes tears flow out our eyes we try to hold them inside but everyone has to cry. Even a man it's a way of life understand that crying lets out stress if we just let tears will be met. Don't regret a tear have no fear everyone cry's here. Can you hear someone cry? We all cry at funerals when someone close dies but it's ok to let it out just cry.

40. Sad: We all feel down and get sad, but we can get up change our moods God shows us what to do. When stress overcomes you anything can make you sad but it's ok there's another day. Through every dark day, there will be one which shines bright. Just cherish the times u spent the blessings you have love life don't be sad!

41. Treasure: Treasure is more Mirer than gold. I treasure the bible the stories told. I want you all to know something's you truly treasure you won't let go. There's so much to treasure, yourself every day, and the blessings of God you have received. Treasure it because it won't leave we treasure are family, friends, Girlfriends, and wife. Throughout our lives I wish we could treasure more. It isn't about what you can afford but morally what you value and what you hold together. It's a way of life and every day we treasure.

42. Wrongs from rights: We shall evidentially all know our wrongs from rights. Every cause has an effect the life you select the decisions you make is the consequences you select, It's wrongs from rights. Every day we make mistakes every day we make choices ignore those voices. Then to yourself, the best way to handle this situation comes rightful anticipation of being alright. We got to know in this life our wrong from rights.

43. Listen and learn: Listen to learn what you will earn is more than a lesson but a blessing, of ourselves. Listen to God but barely anybody else. Take advice and take from it what u know is right. We all want to learn as much as possible but listen because without you can't learn to overcome obstacles. Life can suck you in like a Popsicle life runs like a bicycle. Every person through life will get their turn through it but we must listen and learn.

44. The life we are facing: People don't understand the world and their placement. I ask you to look at the life you are facing? Rather it's succeeding to Heaven or to Hell, not in jail and our destiny would fail. God is our living recipe something we desperately need but throughout life what we will accomplish learn and receive. When we leave they're only two placements. Just look at the life we are facing.

45. Memories: The times we forever treasure in our hearts. Memories that keep us from falling apart. I mean where can I start I have many memories. Some good, some when I was mad, some that were bad, and some that make me sad. Throughout all those times we shall cherish all the memories we have. It's what keeps a smile on your face, how you remember friends, and you hold it all to the end. Without it left empty living on this place to be free. I shall always hold my precious memories.

46. Each step you take: Each step you take regulates your living fate. I pray I soon will be able to step through Heaven's gate. Each and every day as you take a breath you take constant steps. You have to accept what's in stored walking out that door. There's things to do and a lot more. You have legs to walk for your own purpose. Rather its school work or home just be careful where you step for it could be wrong. It's easy to be misplaced. Do what God say's walk by faith, not by sight. Follow me step by step I'll lead you through those gates. The world is not safe so please watch each step you take.

47. In heaven: Dear God, I ask you today what it will be like in Heaven? Is it colorful never ending and wonderful? Is there infinite things to do, or you have a plan for everyone as they move? Do we sit, do we sleep, and do we eat? Is there days months or weeks? Do we talk do we speak are we angels or spirits? What do we learn living life fully under you in Heaven the gift we may earn? I don't know what it's like where it is at but I hope to you my spirit fly back. Does it stay open 24/7 like 7/11? Dear lord, please tell me what it's like in heaven?

48. When the sun rises: When the sun rises, every day brings more surprises. What we are not realizing is that there is only one sun and one moon. Soon as the night is away the sun rises and resumes, bringing light to you. There is so much to do and so much to see and a lot is make believe. When you wake and leave aren't we all wishing for is peace, never the lease we walk the streets on our normal schedule trying to avoid the Devil. God has a life living plan and multiple surprises when the sun rises.

49. When you find love: When you find love it's hard to let go. When it's true love you will know. Sometimes you find it slow sometimes fast. We all know throughout our past love can end fast. It Can have you sad, broken you gave your heart like a token. How would you know if that person is joking? You will never find perfect so keep hoping, keep searching, scoping, but when you find it you feel at ease. You follow that journey take a seat. The fire that you make together can you feel the heat? You look at that person like never before you finally received that key to that closed door. When you find love there comes more. Marriage perhaps a family tree the right one for your destiny. If it's real you want nothing above. Just how it is when you find love.

50. Pride: Something that grows on you through life is pride. It's not about what you decide but how your heart deprives. You realize deep inside lies pride. So hard to earn, one day it will come to your turn. Pride you will earn something more than to learn. It's more than care pride we share forever you will glide once you hold pride.

51. Mistakes: Something we make every day is mistakes. From the choices you make for situations you're in and how you take. Just relax and wait think with hope react with faith it's never too late. We all learn from our mistakes it's turns you into a better person. We are only human so it's uncertain if the mistakes you make aren't hurting. It brings a lesson regret but we all are truly blessed for the choices we make but each choice may bring mistakes.

52. To be a mother: No other but a woman has what it take to be a mother. The sacrifices they take. The stress they suffer just makes them tougher. Do you ever wonder the job of being a mother? Raising a family birthing kids. Oh, how precious it is to experience the life they live. Look at it from a different point of view, the impact it can do to you. Some choose to give up have an abortion. That child they have lost but the pain will catch up with you. No one but God and experiences of others know's what it like to be a mother.

53. Enjoy it while it last: Life is too short ends way too fast. My advice to you is to enjoy it while it lasts. Your memories your childhood the future the past the times you had, the good times, and laughs. We only live one life I just want to live it right. I don't know what's in stored the man I will become but I hope it's fun I shall cherish each moment I have so my motto is to enjoy it while it last.

54. Pain: Throughout life we must never take the lord in vain. For the Devil brings pain life isn't a game. We suffer and hope for change. It's not stressing you're not going insane. Without pain, it's not just hurting bleeding abused and screaming. It's what we learn to experience and come over. In this life, we go through a lot. Hell is a place that's too hot. The Devil provokes you to rot. Oh, when will it stop? The stress the agony and it's never the same. Someday we all will experience pain.

55. Don't cry: Don't cry God has a plan. Don't cry you will find the right woman or man. There's hope God is are helping hand don't cry you can be forgiven. Just know there are consequences for each decision. Don't cry we all someday must die. Don't you realize that person has reached the other side? Keep ya head up wipe them tears dry them eyes. Every little thing going to be alright don't cry.

56. Patience: I know you got dreams keep chasing. Everything takes time have patience. It's More than waiting just look at the big picture accept the life we are facing. Stop rushing why are you racing? God's got a plan and placement. We shall all going to Heaven just have patience.

57. A purpose: There's a purpose why things happen. I know somethings aren't always met for satisfaction. Damn, look at your reaction. Keep striving and trying, keep climbing. Almost everything consists of timing. Have no fears God is close he's here. One day the Devil will disappear. God created us all this world, this surface. He did everything for a purpose.

58. A lesson: A lesson is a blessing, it's something we learn from. A mistake and a lesson are learned. A lesson can be in school or a moment of time something really impacted you. We know why we shouldn't go for that action again. That's when the lesson begins, for example, a thing hard not to do is sin. In the end, comes that question throughout life and each blessing did you learn a lesson?

59. You realized: There comes a time when you get caught in life or a situation by surprise. You then realized that you could have did something different gave things a different try. You ask yourself why? You might regret but you have to respect that sometimes thing just happens for reasons, that we can't control. The life we live we just don't know how to be perfect. Something's doesn't show, you ever went through something in your life and wrongly criticized that person place at that time? It then slips your mind that you find it wasn't a lie that person did try. Déjà vu hits you by surprise you ask God why? The answers come out and you realized.

60. A moment of time: Life goes by fast. There comes a moment of time to strive and recognize. Tomorrow is not promised any second you can die. That moment of hope to God you fly. A moment of time can be we when you commit a crime. When you wrote a rhyme when you flipped a dime? It was misled heads instead. You wish and shall try to accomplish what you really need your main goal and dream. There's a moment of time when God will show you, you don't need anything for he is our king just relax be under his wings. What that means every day you will run into and find a moment of time.

61. Never give up: They say if you think of someone every day never give up its ok find another way. Every day it's in your mind and won't fade have faith and trust never give up. There comes a time when you give up on God and go through a lot but stand strong and remain tough never give up. For God never gives up on you the world is rude and the Devil awaits for the wrong move. How can we loose and throughout what we do how can we improve? Don't worry about such and such. I know at times enough is enough, but trust in God never give up.

62. I see no ending: Life is an endless dream for some scheme building a false team. I pictured this before again and again there's a two-way road one for Christ and one to sin. I'm only starring looking for a right away day after day I swerve and spin. Thinking to myself how can one stay straight? Walking down the line of fate gaining a key to Heaven's gate. At times I hallucinate seeing the angels that would abide. Seeing the end of my demise seeing the rain, cupid crying eyes. Seeing Adam and eve descending to we. What shall I see? I looked in the mirror closed my eyes then fraternized. It's dark as I pray to God hoping he provides hope, which is light. Hopefully a sign or message intercepted to me he will be sending. I look at the world in my eyes and see no ending.

63. Tupac (Pac means peace) Dear Tupac: The way you rhymed and on beats how perfectly your flows was timed. No one can do it like Pac in his prim.   . I don't know what was going through your mind. The way you expressed yourself through every rhyme was crazy. You reached to the streets the dying breed and babies. You talk about hate towards the police. Man, I don't know you personally, but I know you had the rapping ability and wrote poetry that I couldn't believe I've heard and seen. It took me time to realize who you somewhat was the type of guy the thug life you lived. Man, Pac no one can rap better than you and probably haven't experienced what you went through and did. You were blessed and you did accept that all there was in the streets was death people dying till no one was left. I honestly don't know if you are still alive if that day you got shot again died Makaveli I hope you're really alive? Because the message of your name is telling me I am alive. Why did people want to put you away? Was it the freemasons and Illuminati? You don't know me but, know I'm a fan and understand if you are gone rest in peace. In fact, rap is Pac you never did stop. Please don't take this wrong but rap changed ever since you been gone. I hope the person that shot u last rot and you my idle Tupac!

64.   When will there be change: As time moves on and days still feel the same? Throughout all the things we go through all the pain. When will there be change? I learned that life isn't a game but who could complain we loose and sometimes we gain. When things go wrong we are quick to blame someone else. So many people crying out for help and people with so much wealth only focus on themselves. We wait for change, have many discussions and through the pain still no justice. Where is the helping hand? When Obama got elected he said "Yes we can" look back to Malcolm x, Martin Luther king, All the people fighting forming a team. Through blessings through laws and amendments help from presidents. We all are equal supposed to be treated the same but when will there be change?

65.   Smile: Smile cause you're here have no fear God is near. Soon the stress will disappear and a smile on your face will appear. Smile because you're happy and living we smile when we have a good feeling. We smile around family and friends like those childhood memories back when you were 10. All those memories keep us from being empty. Sometimes it's hard to smile maybe because you feel you have low confidence in yourself. You put makeup on your image it's concealed but God will show that your beauty is real. Smile don't hold a frown the Devil can't forever hold you down. You can change yourself through God right now, so smile.

66. The world is crazy: The world is crazy, have you read the newspaper or check the news lately? Everyday chaos seems to be awaiting. From people who die to suicide, their own life there taking. In God's kingdom forsaken. It just amazes me the world is crazy. Every day people commit crimes killing doing homicides, the life everyday people face. Kidnaping among kids girls getting rape. How can we feel safe when more trouble loses faith? I ask God why is the place for us to stay until our destiny. The Devil is lurking hurting doing others shady. God damn the world is crazy!

67. A gift: A gift is a blessing from God. With this gift may you accomplish a lot? We are all talented different a lot the same, different names and a lot chase fame. We give everything to reach our dream. From plain constant working building a team. With that gift your blessed with it's a proof that God exists. You can achieve believe but don't quit. We have some type of special gift. It's not like we already know and predict. The message to you all God blessed all of us with a gift.

68. The key to that closed door: I walk up so many steps and many more. I'm in this world searching for the key to that closed door. I don't know exactly what I'm here for? But I better myself and strive to do more. Sometimes I'm too blind to see what's right in front of me. If I don't pick it up I'd probably leave it could have been underneath my feet. Maybe the hill is too steep. I'm sleep in a dream still seeing my everyday reality. My spirituality lurks for God and his presence his lessons and blessings. To strength my everyday existence. So I'm back searching what I'm looking for. I see so many doors, but there not all met for me. Then I get lead to a set of many of keys. I don't know which one fits and what door to open. I get on my knees and pray for a moment "dear Lord, I love you, you give me hope and faith. I wait and I ask God can you please lead me the way? I hold in my hand multiple keys to my destiny but which door is the right path which key is the recipe? To be lead where we will one day meet? I don't want to open the wrong door and experience heat. I ask can you lead me to you. In time it will come true I'll figure out my purpose here what I'm looking for? I then find the key to that closed door!

69. Don't judge a book by its cover: Don't judge a book by its cover. Looks can be deceiving and undercover. The assumption of that first look will have you ''shook'' like a pointed out crook. A lot of people go off one day but believe in God he will show you the way like when you conversate. Then feelings for that person in time escalate. Times moves on things get straight. So as people we can only go with the moment and play. From times that were good with laughter then comes, days and days of chapters. Maybe in our eyes an illusion then it all comes faster resolution to a conclusion. That's when we get our life back then hit's the climax. The truth comes back, you take another look then things recover. Don't judge a book by its cover!

70. I miss: I miss old memories. Times went by so fast I miss my past the life I had. Makes me sad and flashbacks make me mad. I know we think back just a puppet in this life, strings attached. Some lucky a lotto ticket just scratched. I miss just looking back on the road in this life looking for signs. I miss times all left behind I find my mind and feeling in the abyss. Oh, how I wish I could go back in the day fix my flaws and all my mistakes. I miss people times was good just up to no good. Wondering at a young age in a stage of feelings that faded away. Now I look to recover another day. For all those parents that died, you probably wish you kiss. A lifelong lists, I miss.

71. Fame: Life's a big competition and game. It seems we all search for fame. To let the world know our names. We get tired of living plain we strive for change and begin chasing for fame, but once you get it you won't be the same. You go through life seeing what's happening but money can't buy you happiness. It then brings sadness and madness. Some this, some that, actors and actress finally reach their dreams gave up everything then they feel odd it isn't what it seems. They get cocky but then hits the media, industry, and paparazzi. Its part of the game, so be careful and know what's going to happen once you reach fame.

72. Let the moment play: As we go through days sometimes you feel things have changed. From a better state, you conversate try to relax and wait. Just have patience let the moment play, God will show you the way. Times will come out real in time the truth will reveal. You then get over that steep hill. there're a lot of bumps in this road. Perfection we don't know but take each step slow let life lead you the way. Just let the moment play.

73. Sunset: The sunset rises in the east and sets in the west. May we shine but we are too blind in this quest. The light brings heat but our eye can only see what's make believe. The beauty of the sunset brings much color the clouds. If you get a chance catch it, watch it set as you lay down the sunset brings a smile. It happens at a certain time the picture of that sunset won't leave your mind. You then find that we are truly blessed for that moment to be caught. May we treasure each sunset.

74. Segregation: The bad time of the black race was segregation treated wrongfully in any placement. Did those slaves deserve the pain they went through? Treated cruel and everyday suffered. I thought we were treated all equal. Those people were beaten killed mistreated serving others people who didn't care different races treated unfairly. They did stand together for "change" but throughout most of it, no change. Perceived wrong because the color of their skin tone. I know its history and morally gone but how did people feel throughout this dictation? That's why it's hard to be black looking back to segregation.

75.   A chance: Everyone deserves a chance for love romance and God's plan. With a chance maybe we can it's a world that awaits anything to happen. With a chance comes maybe satisfaction but our reaction is we need it right there and then. There will be another chance don't rush just trust that we all experience enough. When times is rough stand tough you will see things come again we all get a chance.

76.   Will you let go: When that person hurts you the most will you let go or lose control and think there's more to go? You then go with the flow in this life you got to be strong. You only know what you truly lost when that person is gone. When the person is around you change your tone feeling eased at home. There's a lot of things for you to try and forever hold. Thinking without you're cold? From family to friends and foes to how you're living. When will you give that person a chance? They will be forgiven it's hard to make that decision. Time will tell we don't know but when will you let go?

77.   As I walk through the valley the shadows of deaths: What is my fate if I shall die before I wake in those gates would I make? As I walk through the valley the shadows of deaths I hope God regulates my every calculated step and not left in this world till nobody is left. I feel without God and my bible defile thoughts of going suicidal. I am selfish only want what I know but I got to live in the moment and enjoy the flow. Dear God hold me close don't let go cause all I fear hear is the Devil. If I don't listen my vision is seeing me killed or in prison. The world's full of hate, competition, and everyday people go missing to stay alive I kept wishing. Heaven hopefully my destiny but I am too blind to see what's behind me and every memory is rewinding. I feel at the top still climbing searching but not finding. I feel as if I am blessed I wonder why Jesus wept and why in the east the sunsets and what comes next. When I rest and my spirit has left to God shall I resurrect? What do I do as I walk through the valley the shadows of deaths?

78.   Before I die: I ask to those that around to only pray to God make no sound smile don't frown, God, I will have found. Now that I am in the present and still alive I wonder every day what will I do or say before I die? I can't lie I'm not a perfect guy but every day I shall try to rightfully be recognized by the world every woman and guy. Just know hold your pride listen to my words of the wise live your life right because any second something can catch you by surprise. I beg you all to not commit suicide go to hell and rot this life this family these real friends and God is all you got. God has a plan for you and a plot to reserve you in eaven save a spot. I pray I shall fly you shall not cry life's goes on and days go by don't wonder why for my time is up I shall stand tough. I know life is rough I hate that I've sinned but lord I beg you to let me in!

79. It ain't easy being free: There comes a time in a stage when we are down and caged, played filled with rage. Those out on the streets, quick to commit a felony. That would mean the Devil got over thee or me. Man, it ain't easy being free to all of us, every life's unquestioning seize to be more than a dream, reality. Seems the world is ugly and mean no longer kings and queens. Even now it isn't what it seems I mean you could be in the wrong place and wrong time and find you are around a person that committed a crime. Now you find from being around you have to do time. Some rather die than be trapped in jail. Some say it's a living hell, writing letters of mail but what can you tell. The world is designed for every human being to fail. Only time will tell but do you feel what I feel? Do you see what I see? It ain't easy being free.

80. Empty: Empty is hollow you swallow but still can hold your sorrows. Empty today maybe tomorrow. What do I do what do I follow? I have been through plenty and still left empty. When shall there be providers I feel then no memories old timers. I have no reasoning for this place going off my race the life we all face is filled with hate, disgrace. The mind is a terrible thing to waste. God then displays my own fate. I shall not feel safe here God please appear, make the Devil disappear. Fulfill my dreams come into me take me away leave me empty.

81. Accept: I accept who I am and where I stand as a man I have many dreams but forwardly is God plan. It all begins and I accept that I've sinned I try to break that cycle saying not again but that is pretend till I get over my flaws. When it's the end of my demise I will accept God's call. I know I'm only human and at times will fall but I stand tall and fear no man. As I accept anything in this world I can achieve there is a God I accept and believe. I hope when I leave you will all remember me. Who I am what I've done the journey I took and the man I've become. There're a lot of things that we don't want to believe act naïve and our eye is too blind to see what's right in front of all of we. Don't ignore those signs you'd be impressed. If you let the main thing that connects, everything we must accept.

82. Stabbed you in the back: It's a lifelong fact it's hard to trust because anyone can stab you in the back. People can be fake just wait and the true colors will reveal. The person might bear to kill look to steal how would you feel? If it wasn't the person you would least expect the most that special friend that was close would try to sink your boat. Took all of your things your life jacket so you couldn't float. How would you react and that person you would probably subtract because people wait to attack. To take what they think is there's back act fake put on a big act. It's a fact that karma will strive back, hit them with a whack. How would you feel if someone stabbed you in the back?

83. A Negro: Looked at with racism and perceived to accomplish zero. When people look at a black person they call them a Negro, a monkey, and slave. That's the way our race is looked at every single day. Some do respect and can connect but life's set so every black male or female to be misjudged and fail. As a person how can we prevail ''How is he black, look as his skin tone you can tell I hope that negro goes straight to hell and rot why don't you all disappear you don't belong here'' They don't seem to care aren't we made equal but treated unfairly. I know God cares he brought us here. Nowadays a Negro accomplish a lot from Jacky Robinson to Tupac to many it don't stop. We don't care if you don't like us but trust we fight and are tough through history we have been through enough. I believe we are all hero's, I'm proud to be a Negro!

84. Survive: When are close to the end and feel we will die there comes hope to survive. I dedicate this to all but morally a few. Throughout holocaust the surviving Jews. Forced to work beaten experiencing torture and put in camps killed off. The enemies with Hitler did it and felt fulfilling and they took lives of over 6 million. I can't imagine the pain they suffered like no other a lot died cried but some strive and did survive. I remember a holocausts survivor coming to my school and told all of us her story. She believed in God and reached all glory. The first thing she said that stood out to me the guard told her to say she was 18 and she didn't die. Right, then her mom and sisters left she never saw them again. She worked in factories and actually stayed alive. That's when I closed my eyes damn near cried and realized throughout anything with God rightfully on our side hoping and showing faith every night. Through it all in any situation when you know you're about to die no lie just strive and you will recognize we can survive.

85. Sex: A spiritual feeling too deeply connect is sex, flesh on flesh. You would never guess how things change with another after sex. It puts babies in a carriage By God sex is made for marriage. People don't understand it's God's plan and made for a man and woman. You then feel fulfilling one in a million. You won't feel the same for that person after. That moment you would catcher more than memories filled with laughter but it's a disease that can turn you worse than feigns. If only we knew it's met for your queen but life is poisoned won't rest. It's a mess. Now people just have sex.

86. Having a baby: If you see what I see we do believe you change once she is having a baby. A lot become parents and are happy some don't want to believe and are quick to leave but it's meant to be. For others now parents a father a mother you smile. As you know you're going to hold a precious child someone's probably having one it's happening right now. The mother holds that child for 9 months or before through birth there closer than the father. Being a mother is harder it can drive you crazy. It just what happens in life if your body is ready. You have planted that seed she's having a baby.

87. Pregnant: To every girl it does exist it is easy to get pregnant. Even if your selection uses perfection. Sometimes that other percent brings a good chance girls won't even choose to pick but they will know once they begin getting sick you pee on a stick. The results come back your pregnant. You won't know the gender till it's time boy or girl but you're bringing a blessing to this world. It's very important don't poison that seed and have an abortion take a life that isn't right. How do you think you were born your mom's wounds were torn. Now kids are hard to afford but you will have dozens of memories and many more. Just a gift in time you will get pregnant.

88. Style: Style is a passion for fashion how you prepare yourself is another's reaction. Everyone strives for satisfaction some don't care style there lacking. From makeup shoes and clothes it all sums up to his or her style of flow. From classy, casual, presidential, style tells a lot of info. Scan and analyze something different will come off into your mind you're no longer blind. Then look from the head all the way down do you see their style?

89. Help is on the way: If you are in need and every day you pray don't worry help is on the way. It might not take a day but just wait with every dark night comes a bright day. The pain will then fade just listen to God when you pray that's the only way. You can't do it all by yourself if we all at times need help. We must everyday hope have faith throughout the way we conversate. Don't worry help is on the way.

90. Trust: it's hard to discuss on a subject like trust. We are constantly going through enough. People seem to bluff in my eyes I only see my family true friends and God watching over me. How can this be people are always changing on us. You never know who's real till the truth spills it's how I feel. Watch who's around you there quick to turn and kill I don't like to rush I think on such and such and hush don't you think to yourself every day who could we trust?

91. As you close your eyes: As you close your eyes what lies inside your mind anything unusual you find? Do you feel what's around you? Do you hear time?

Seconds are multiplying just near pear silence. Then comes violence to sirens. What is your naked eye applying? What you see you're realizing. Do you close your eyes when you relax sleep and lay or when you pray? At that time what do you say what lies insides those close blinds? You will be surprised what you really hear, see, and find. As you close your eyes.

92. One day you will come back to me: I woke up without you not knowing what to do it's true I have lost you. I walk outside after waking up from a dream and I see in the sky us. I'm nearly hallucinating cause, in reality, you're no longer around gone my mind recognition but my heart doesn't listen, you I begin missing. Time moved on still I'm tripping I await to find you like yesterday I use my heart as bait and still fishing. I'll let time do its deed I know to me you will succeed you I will actually see. I know one day you will come back to me.

93. One day: Somehow some way I will know everything that I've constantly asked God throughout the times I've prayed. One day I will be on top of my dreams marry my queen have a family tree build a team take care of my family. Let the world see nothing but me. The future comes I have a hint upon destiny. I know God will question me I'll be called to leave. Why am I here? As long as you are near my pride and hope won't disappear. My life is reality more than a dream. I take it each day and step by step God show me the way. I will see you one day!

94. Can't live without: I wake up and pray and remain smiling. I know my road may be overcrowded but the competition brings desire for me. To do better, I try to play smart and stay clever. Every day I shall think bigger chase the spirit of God forever. It's rightful to me my only treasure. I can feel it when where and whatever weather but I go after cheddar. I fly and flock with feathers just me and God together. I hope to climb the tallest mountain and drink the water that's fresh from the fountain. Dear Father more times are accounting but you know your spirit I can't live without it!

95. Mom: Dear Mom, I thank you more than ever because for me you always wanted me to do better. You I treasure most because even though I'm not your own we've been so close. You help me float and known when dangers are ahead seen the most. Sometimes I feel you're like a ghost, just constantly watching over me. You just want me to succeed and not be like others go down the path of others. I love you more than you will ever know. Life's not hitting me like I hoped so it's hard to show I know to you I been special and your own. I think back with flashbacks one day it will rest. Don't forget I will do it all for you because I know you'd do the same for me. You started a lot of this family tree but please let old times that hold you down leave. Ever Since my brother got deployed you been so paranoid. Scared and aware of people watching you there but don't worry you will be ok. I wonder how you get through each day. I must say you have done so much you I mostly trust. I wish I could go back and cherish you better you are the best forever always the bomb I love you, mom.

96. Dad: Dear Dad, It makes me sad looking back because the times we had. A father you kind of lacked not because you weren't doing your job but always gone. I'm not saying you did wrong you brought me in this world, this place. I see you in me every day. When I look back your face in my heart for you I forever have space. Your more than u seen you've blessed all of us with strong genes. I mean if it wasn't for you I wouldn't be here and throughout my memories with you, I know you care. You told me find God live right make money get a job and go to the military. I want you to know that I'm very blessed and have so many talents that you should see and thanks to you I have received. When you die I will cry and be sad but throughout the times, I can always tell you I love you, dad.

97. Another year: One year we hope to accomplish a lot but over time, the results will be brought. The battles you fought the good memories you hold the lessons caught. Things you earn lesson you have taught. Some years are the best some sad but cherish those times you have. Don't worry you're still here there is more time and another year.

98. Birthday: We all wake up with a tremendous same. Just a yearly blessings you get together with family receiving smile why because it's that special day, your birthday. The day you were brought into this world. You get older and change but still you feel the same. Just a yearly blessing you get together with your family receiving presents. How do you feel as they sing to you it's your special day? What shall you do make a lists? Then at the end make a wish. It's for you nobody else watches, as those candles go away and melt. Each time you don't forget you treat It a special way on your birthday.

99. The rain that helped the flowers grow: It was dry and drought as can be. It seems that God hasn't shed a tear for thee. It hasn't rained how could this be? How can farmers plant their seeds? That would give them vegetables and more money they shall receive. Heat, heat go away let it rain and cool the day. There's plenty sunlight but the flowers need more water is all they ask for. The seeds are planted for the flowers to start to grow. The light hits the color change they seem to glow. How would you know? That's the rain that helped the flowers grow.

100. I'll warm you when you're cold: As we walk outside I'm with you tonight. I feel your body running my fingers down your skin and feel goose bumps. Just sit and take my jacket your cold quit acting, don't front. I'll do it all for you because I treasure you like Gold. I'll warm you when you're cold.

101. You shine like a star: I've looked at your eyes and realize I seen you before in the sky. It took me time and caught me by surprise, to notice you shine. When I look into your eyes I see the sky at night your pupils circle around like the moon and they glare like the moonlight. I looked outside wide and far. I know exactly where you are because you shine like a star.

102. The future of you and me: I always have these fantasies and dreams, so many visions I see. I want you to picture the future of you and me. Passionately lovers if I have to wait until marriage to be intimate to gain your full trust let it be. Continue to see it out let it come slow your imagination will show our love glow. You will feel something in your soul your heart will beat as you lay beside me staring, glaring, sharing, loving, caring, and growing to be one. I'd always make you laugh we have the most fun. If we had a kid what would you want a daughter or son? The worries will be none. Love will change our hearts cupid's dart would spark before it even start. We shall never again fall apart you have my heart. I'll embrace you we when make love cherish your face without makeup. Take care of you when you're sick calm your nerves when you have a fit, be there through sick and poor in the future the past the pain which last I will restore. Just the two of us holding hands as time flies we will expand the more were together the more I understand. Take my hand it will be ok together we will walk, talk, pray, sleep and kiss. This will all come true with the approval of God granting fates wish. I can see how you would feel as you read I'll always be there and in need you, I would feed thank God for you yes indeed. I can see us planting a seed doing God's deed many great things will lead. If you were hurt my heart would bleed. If you were sad I'd be mad if it were my bad I promise to fix it that feeling of us two makes me feel glad. I'd thank God for every moment we have, when were old my love won't dwindle beautiful you're my gold I'll warm you when it's cold. You I must hold if truth be told my honesty won't fold. Your smile is special to me your soul gives me temptation of ecstasy. Feelings will be beyond a mountains peak hear me as I speak. Right now without I'm weak it is you I only want and seek. If I die I pray all the poems I've written to you, you keep I pray you dream of me as you sleep. Memories of nothing but love so bittersweet. Due to fate, you're my soul mate an everlasting date I pray it isn't too late. For once take away the hate open your eyes visualize and actually see the future of you and me.

103. This vision: Sometimes I dream images that turn to visions. If I don't fully listen to God I see me in prison or dead. ''follow me step by step'' is what God said I'm still imagining and getting lead to one decision. What will I have done to become the real me? I've overlooked my destiny. I'm no longer blind there's nothing missing. I've seen and recognition, this vision.

104. When I thread the needle in my skin: when I thread the needle in my skin. I try to stop the bleeding of times I've sinned. That's when it begins I no longer pretend I accept salvation again. Then God is my only true friend to help me get closer that moment we get closer. You take the weight off my shoulders. I'm not perfect and met to sin but that's when the guilt comes the pain begin. I tell myself never again. That's when I thread the needle in my skin.

105. Pressure: oh why do u want so much of me, is this how it's supposed to be? I search desperately for any opportunities all I see in the community is pressure but not us standing together for the better. A fact that people do whatever they hear whatever they see. Have you watch the news lately? Have you seen what's been going on recently? Why do you think people commit felonies because they believe at the time that was the best thing? Where does it lead in prison, killed, and reminiscing? For that mistake and choice just the pressure of a moment of time hearing that voice, we wish we could rejoice. Some of our flaws the consequences we knew and saw. We must obey the law but some forced, beaten. With others not wanting, but having to work together its life, every day brings pressure.

106. Freedom: Finally, we can walk the streets and freedom we keep. Doesn't mean there will be peace even if we are protected and serve by the police. There're plenty amendments to help us but I ask you all what do you see? Especially when we are attacked by our nationalities. It seems to me we can walk and free to talk but the fed's do stalk. Once you commit crimes and they find it was your fault. The government bare to share a little bit and show so little care but still it's unfair. Look what has happened what we become justice still none. One thing I'm proud to say we have freedom.

107. In America: The home of the brave in America I'm proud to stay because there is freedom and open opportunities. A place where we can be we and feel set free. The flag of stars with, 50. A lot of countries and cities a much good site to see. The place to follow your dreams you can do anything. Strive for much and etc. In America.

108. Forever: For millenniums and more, the Bible preps every human being. For inside and out that door explains who you are what to live for. One thing that we always will treasure is a bible forever.

109. There's no place like home: When were out there for long and gone I know you know there's no place like home. The place where I belong and where I could do no wrong. May friends come along to my sanctuary where I'm rightfully in my zone? Man, there's no place like home.

110. God's gift to earth: You are me I live in you. Yes, it is true once you get birth it's God's gift to Earth. Every day I search for a planted seed without my fantasy I'm left empty. I get many blessing but wait for that special present that's precious. I would love to see it unwrapped by the nurse. Here comes a God's gift to Earth.

111. Have no fear: As I walk through here I'm sincere. Have no fear God is here. No one ever can conceal my spirit but my savior, I await to be hearing I fear no man and have very little friends. I stay calm and pray not to be scared living here God replies ''my son have no fear I am here have no fear''

112. It's never too late: I know it's hard to change for some are not the same. I know you want something most and if you think about it every day don't let go! If things are met to be you will meet again through fate. To find your mate or get through that gate. It's never too late.

113. 3 real chances for love: One after another but no love seems real like a mother. You wait and wait for the right soul mate. You go on many dates and only 3 is real. Those ones you will really feel there's no rush but trust with much as you discuss. The one you are with and fuss with the ones that don't leave and quit. One of those 3 real chances you will see. Believe me, it isn't easy moving on. You begin frozen as you stare feeling lost and wrong. You search through all of the above. You only get 3 real chances for love.

114. Out that door: Look how life's in stored, walking right out that door. It's the wealthy, rich, poor, and so many more. That others can afford it's the real world, no longer a dream but reality out there seems to be different, full of pure competition. It's what we're living for to accomplish many things and many more. It all comes true out that door.

115. Breakaway: So lost stuck in a maze in a stage of rage. How do I past this and get to the last page? When do I ever find the right way to get out? Nothing happens when I scream or shout. I have no more doubts I have to create a new route. To figure out why I'm trapped and what's this about. I ask God to lead the way because I'm stuck in misery every single day. I just pray somehow I will break away.

116. Take my hand: Look into my eyes what do you see? Me fantasizing about you in my dreams. My dear queen can't nothing come between us. Just trust I'm in no rush but I do blush when I'm standing right in front of my crush. I've followed your every footstep to be sure in your heart I'm kept. Once you accept it's God's plan. Just know I'm your number 1 fan. It will be ok everyday just take my hand.

117. When a flower blooms: When a flower blooms it stands out. It finally has grown, overcame the drought. Step by step things change and rearrange. The flower is no longer the same. Now we can take it pass it to another a mother or lover. Just look further time zooms. It stands out when a flower blooms.

118. Buried: Ashes to ashes dust to dust. No need to discuss but Heaven ain't hard to find. Let the pain out your heart clear your mind. It's going to take time. Please, each funeral is necessary. No more misery no more pain. Without that person no longer the same. I ask the lord to spare me. I know how it is when that casket you have to carry. It's part of life were either cremated or buried.

119. Do you care: A lot is constantly going on but how much of it is wrong? Do you see what's hurting everybody? From cities, countries, states, and communities. It's not just you and me it's we. All I see is the world full of fools. Just wanting to be watched on the news. It's not stopping. Always remember somebody is watching. These crimes committed are not forgotten. It's all unfair to walk around and not share not spare. When people are begging over there. We swear help is here but I ask you all do you care?

120. A sign: I walk and search but still haven't found. I look around and see nothing to help. I ask myself, what is it I can't see? What is it for me? No matter what I do I still feel I haven't found a clue. God that's when I pray to you. Asking questions and in time answers, I hope to find? I am losing my mind but can't move as fast as time. All I ask for is a sign.

121. Deep in the blue sea: As the waves pass, just as days in the sea. I swim and lay day by day. Waiting to be saved still haven't found a clue to ever get rescued. I look at the water it is blue, Underneath my feet, it's so cold and deep. I do not scream shout or weep. I wait for what time has for me. I then actually go under water, to see which fish I could eat but then a shark would eat me. I ask for help but haven't found out I am left like a fool. How could this be? I swim for eternity deep in the blue sea.

122. Family: we will die for another cry for another. We help each other, my sisters, and brothers, my wife, my lover. When I'm down you bring me up help me stand strong and remain tough. Everything and anything we will discuss. The light brings out the darker and blood is thicker than water. You strive me to better we are placed in this family tree forever. I remember my past memories when we laugh. I'm too blind to see I must cherish you all. Not just blood friend's people that will be there till the end. We all have the same father can't you see? We are one big family.

123. An addiction: Dear fans, I want you to understand we all have addictions. It's not like we can put cream on it and stop the itching. Don't need to mention I've tried to stop fishing. My minds the bait every day I try not but my mind slips away. Damn, even when I pray it doesn't go away. Can't be around others because it's still will rub off after I saw. I knew it couldn't fall the addiction again called. Even with a genie and wishes, I still see I can't do any different. Dear world I have an addiction.

124. The older we get: The more we age, the older we get. More of life brings a chance person. We overcome burdens no longer hurting. For certain adapted to the way of life. The older we get the more you want to make things right. Life is too short and passes by too fast. We enjoy it while it lasts. Now it begins sadly that we get closer and closer to the end. Trying not to sin and Heaven gate fit in. We being perfect is not a word to go off. May we constantly fix ourselves and help who were with. Don't you see what's ahead as the older we get?

125. Connection: The chemical feelings in your spirit. Once you get near it may be caught in a look. That connection at site with each other you took. A connection is like a book from what you are after. Memories of laughter then days go by like chapters. Something starts an illusion maybe strategizing. Then comes dreams caught by a surprise. Those feeling inside rising like a sunrise. It overruns down love reacts if not subtract then hits the climax. You will sleep with each other like a night cap. Love and attention then comes the connection.

126. Words don't go too far: I know who you are you shine like a star. If it were dark I ask the moon to let the sun appear. The air and trees would give a breeze to travel where you are but we both know words don't go too far. They travel and shall be heard every word pronoun adjective and verb. Sometimes there's a crack in that curve. How can it be fixed? Oh, how we wish and predict but reality were stuck with. When shall love change our hearts? How can another fix this puzzle connect the pieces back apart? Do words actually touch a heart? Can it cure a soul? When we are insecure about ourselves from connecting hitting a goal. We breathe air oxygen is free of toll. Once the dice rolls the stats will arrive at an eye at night. What do you see in the sky? Only with actions of a star, the sun couldn't travel by a car. So words don't go too far.

127. Only God can judge me: Damn, I hate the way you all look. Don't judge a cover by its book and outcast me a crook. I am me you are you I do me and you do you, it's true you don't know me or have a clue. Why wrongly perceive me and act rude? I'm young but not a fool. Glad to say I graduated high school and through the time there I just did me and didn't care. Life's unfair I'm aware but beware. God's got a destine plan for me. For those quick to judge can't call me ugly. To everyone in the world, only God can judge me.

128. The world we pollute: This is to the world I salute. Truth be told we need to do more and recruit stop trashing the world. To every man and woman boy or girl. There needs to be a change in our states and countries can't you see? What we are doing nothing but polluting. What are we pursuing? The cleaner the world is the longer we will live. Show that Mother Nature exists. From wars to people robbing stores. What is this for? In the end, it's we that's going to lose. Look you fools don't you see the world we pollute?

129. Women: Made from a man what people don't understand is women are created to listen to a man. It's God's plan and there is someone out there made exactly for you. It's true women are beautiful creatures on Earth but men don't realize how much their worth. Women tend to get hurt and only treated like dessert. They are made to put first realize for every woman comes the right guy. In a matter of experiencing a lot of try's. The reason why I adore women so much is because I trust that these women are more than enough. Don't worry girls I am a good guy and fan. I do see how important you are women.

130. A man without love: Alone without a campaign; a bird with broken wings. No longer a dove a man without love, is a mystery life is put in simplicity. Though tomorrow is not promised. How can we live in happiness? Without something to love and to you honest. A friend is but a shadow and without love seems shallow. A heart can't be at full when hate overwhelms in a duel. A love one opposite of cruel. Someone to pray with day and night. Someone to cherish for eternal life. Soul mates soon in fate to become husband and wife. Day by day night by night. No longer in darkness let there be light! A gift sent from Heaven's above. Until an angel complying reaching full capacity. Living in darkness not knowing what are souls are truly made of, a man without love.

131. Time heals all pain: Once strike you won't feel the same. The lighting strikes then comes dark clouds so you continue to frown. Only in a while, the sun will come out and then will come to a smile. Only a certain time gravity can pull you down. You make no sound because pain is all you found. Hurting your soul heart and flesh. Dear God when will it rest? If you let I guess I'll put the skeletons out my closet and confess. Day by day praying for change going completely insane. Hopefully, things will be tamed because time heals all pain.

132. My soul: The wind blows multiple chills through my soul. I hold on to the door knob but lose control and let go. I'm down a path I don't know. It rains then suddenly it snows. I go with the flow but things glow. If the truth, be told. I pray and pray waiting for my spirit to jump up. I began brave in a stage to forgive and to forget no longer hurting. I'll strive to glide with curiosity of courage. May I walk and jump out the spiritual window and let it all go. Lord forgives me have mercy on my soul.

133. My pen: So committed but still can't fully see. How could this be? Somehow I'm still alright I use my heart to bring out light. Let the ink on the pen ignite together with poetry we will fight. Morning after morning night after night. Despite the bad times, each line I define will fight. I make my own journeys provide my own flight. The ticket is the message I hope to receive. Those that do read please oh please have faith in me. I shall strive to succeed sweat and bleed poetry. All I need is my pin the spirit of God to provide aid and light. I don't need light to write my imaginary friend is my pen. The lyrics it proves and lens. I write more and more like an everyday chore. My mind feels at ease like the waves on the shores perfection I strive for. I'm not the type to always write neatly but my words tell a story. You are the audience so take a seat. I'll take you out of this world lift you off your feet. Imagine you in a dream you're sleep. Then the reality of what you are listening to creeps. The picture in your mind it then feels no longer a game. I'll paint the picture and your memory would hold the frame. Soon you will know my name. Greatness has come we begin friends. I welcome you to the life of my pen.

134. As time flies: As times flies I've realized Life in my eyes. In the truth of all lies time. People were imprisoned in the mind. As time flies I hope to find more signs. As a world, we are divine but to reality blind. Many retrospects to the past behind. Many try to seek an eye out the blinds enemy lines. As time flies many will commit crimes. We chance situations with stipulations of getting tails on a dime. Tails never fail heads which lead to many mistakes. As time flies people will be fruitful and multiply. Due to time, we all one day will die. As time fly's by more presidents will come. When will fate be done? The troubles none a question to you and me. What do we want out of life? To be one with Jesus Christ? A family perhaps a husband or wife? As time flies will we strategize, compromise, and hold our pride inside? Many days of sunrise minutes multiply. Many memories and times that we cried many times we lied. Many causes for effects for the choices we select karma resurrects. As time flies we shall be gravitating speaking out the truth for the youth and elaborating. Why put each other down? Try congratulating times are awaiting were contemplating. Many struggle to survive due to their occupation. As time is racing take the time to solve the equation of the life we are facing. Stressing back and forth pacing. I have a pledge for, the nation. Some only reach success and the rest are chasing. I think it's time to bow our heads and pray thank the Lord every day. Before we lay down and look out see what I found. He is the only king that shall be crowned. I hope we all float in the sea and thee don't drown. One day you will look at the ocean and see it's not dry. One day you will look and see the sun has an eye. The clock of existence of you and I as we will soon die. More generations come alive. Descending between you and I, as time flies.

135. The sky: the sky defines the weather deep inside. The routes of the clouds are where the stars are found. The rain pours and then comes more. The sun beams the sky with all is one big team. The clouds are frozen mold when it's very cold. Look out below then comes the snow. When the clouds are foggy and dark lighting may start. Man, I wish I could have visited the site. Just fly very high to see the sky.

136. The Industry: The success placement in our dreams that has evolved through centuries the industry. The business behind the scenes on the big screen there are different industries but mainly fame for life in this game is like monopoly having our dreams sold as property. There is a small chance we can be anything but the reality of the industry is the after effects some people become rich then fall into depth. Sometimes bad luck you catch fame isn't always met. You must know what you are getting yourself into. There's only so many ways to win but too many ways to lose in the industry you have much to prove and every step is calculated, every move. Some look at the industry and get confused. Be careful on the path you choose nothing is easy and along with everything people change in the industry.

137. Why envy me: Why envy me Show hate racism. Calling me a Negro a monkey judging me calling me ugly. You just don't see who I am what I can be. If you took time got to know me. You would know my lifestyle isn't easy. Don't judge me by my face the cover of the book. Just because I'm young and black outlaw me a crook giving me a dirty look. Damn, I just want to be accepted not arrested mistreated because I'm talented but conceited. Only in Cod, I'm believing can't you see? So why envy me.

138. Have mercy on us: As a citizen, I've realized that we constantly get terrorized. From school shooting to bombings at certain places. Just different faces of what lies ahead. Some scared to sleep in their bed because instead shot in the head. Why is there so much chaos? Can't it just be peace no more wars reached? If I have the right to speak. Why battered and bruised? The more we lose. Fools not even money can barely help us. In God, we trust please Lord have mercy on us.

139.   My imaginary friend: Nobody sees you no even me for you live in me. I know one day I'll understand how much you are of a helping hand. You're nearly visible but not to my naked eye. For at times you will catch me by surprise. I always wonder why you I can't seem to find. It seems uncertain you truly are perfect and getting closer to you is worth it. Just getting that makes me nervous. I know one day you will be visible to my eye. I then stop not even to think to sin. You ride by my side till I die till the end. One day I will finally understand. My imaginary friend.

140.   An eye for an eye: Usually the temptation of revenge in the brain. Giving hateful anticipation, which strives for hurtful motivation. It's different from karma or let God take care. It's when you don't spare but retaliate just want to get even and catch them there. If I broke your arm your mind would despite brake mine. Not necessarily a crime but you find that all you want is to get back. So you want to react, attack maybe strategize, Catch them by surprise. An eye for an eye.

141.   The mind is a terrible thing to waste: Alcohol, crystal, crack and etc. Which leads to deceive the brain. On this place, just a taste and in moments of time a changed face. A changed heart you're starting to fall apart. Easy to forget but you can't hide. Once place in front of you decide and won't lie. That's when you're back on it and time flies by. People putting things wrongfully in your head. Telling you things that will have you turn up dead. The Devil, Satan, but you need God instead. As I define that a mind is powerful, forceful, and unstoppable. Capable of the impossible but the obstacle is what lands you in the hospitable. Doesn't matter who you are and what race. I want you to know your fate you can separate. The mind is terrible to waste.

142.   Women can be worse than man: I've realized that men aren't the only ones to have selfish needs at times for women this exceeds even though monthly women bleed. It seems sex can be a hobby and because men have their life together women choose to deceive men getting married cheating then get a divorce separate take half of everything and collect child support. Now I'm not talking about all "women" some are faithful but some can be evil. Some women are controlling in a sense they think you they're owing. Back in time women were to vow their man have children be faithful by their side till the end and be the best they can. This generation now has changed to think how important women are and far they have come. Many relationships crumble but all are not men fault women can be crafty, sassy, and playing so many. It seems they use their bodies as a tool to get anything. They take away the true meaning of a woman they lower themselves not knowing what they are worth. I have respect for good women that go to church and not lurk to hurt. Men can be dogs but women can be worse.

143. (Obama)Mr. President: Dear Mr. President living in the white house resident. I feel it's evident that you're black but not relevant. A fact the first president that's black. Proving to our race, there's no pulling back. To the haters how did you react? When you were elected you brought a smile to the whole world. Through your speech, had much to explain. Seems you can bring change you're smart with a good heart. I just hope this country doesn't fall apart and no more wars to start. Well, I got many questions for you. For this country what are you plans to do? How would you pursue change? It's hell here so many on food stamps and welfare. When will it rest? The economy is so much debt. You're a man I do respect. As a Black man, you represent success. I know in the past you've sinned but dear Mr. Obama I fear the world's going to end. Can you bring change? Remember yes we can! From that moment I was your fan. I know you're constantly moving and working for certain. Help the streets something important. I know you aren't perfect and at times nervous but things we shall reach. Man, you have a really good way to say a speech. I just hope you feel this inside? We have to survive and you must stay alive. So what do you decide as the time passes by? To this country, you give our medicine. So bring change Obama, I mean Mr. President.

144. Michael Jackson: Man you are truly the greatest that ever did it. So committed at a young age. Michael, I want to reach out to you in a different way. You see no one really understood you but knew somewhat what you been through. Hip Hop King you could really can sing! I know you're in Heaven. I always wondered how so young at seven years old. You were able to actually follow your dreams, do it all, stay balanced, and you held extraordinary talent. I've always wanted to meet you in person and just ask you questions go back. In fact, just because your skin tone change you were still black. When it happen people didn't know how to react but forget all that. I never realized how much you was judged. Talked down and constantly criticized over your decisions. It's like nobody is perfect. When you died people tried to act like why did we judge him? This and that and I just think you didn't deserve that. The thing I couldn't even measure is how it hurt you. Not anymore I don't care about the things they said you did. I just know you loved kids and hip hop is the life you lived. Living behind closed blinds trying to hide from bad attractions. You are my idle Michael Jackson!

145. One life to live: As I am still alive and exist. I fantasize and predict on future plots. As I stand trapped in this spot. I feel I have to think the best play smart like chess no one I shall impress. The main deed is to succeed and to achieve. I must believe the blessings of God shall I receive. The big competition for recognition fully striving I will complete. I shall stand up constantly on a move no time to take a seat. Unless I build my project for all those that read and see the greatness hidden in me. A kid driven on a journey no looking back to the things I did. No time to regret and reminisce. All those that I miss humble me inside my heart. Spread the pride the world is cursed for you and me. I pray something got to give its how it is. We only get one life to live.

146. Stuck on an elevator: Stuck on an elevator and only two places to go. Up higher or down below. It just me, no phones, no one else, alone. Still I compose myself in my zone. Will I reach up high and get to the other side? Or drop down below rot and fry? What do I decide? How can I strategize? Lord forgive me I apologize! I start to cry. The elevator floor hits I no longer exist and say goodbye. I'm no longer stuck on a hanger. I have left but still my body is stuck in an elevator.

147. Free: As the birds sing, spreads its wings, and fly. Feeling happy inside where to go what to decide? No reason to cry no questions to ask no whys. I shall fly to the east and west, progress to live without stress. Risen and driven to see the life ahead of me. I look for open door opportunities of not to exclude but find a key. Open a path only for me no one shall take me away. As I pray if I shall die before I wake my soul to take. From the Devil, I will escape as God waits. For Heaven, I will soon see then I begin fully free.

148. The stage: The feeling of true bravery just holding a smile. As I look at crowd all surround around me. Too many eyes that lie ahead so all I see is me. Mind over matter paced where I can be fully free. Not in a dream but I only receive the work I put in. I feel so close to this place my true friend which brings so much satisfaction of acting. The journey of it going through each page as I feel amazed. While I'm on the stage!

149. Money can't buy you happiness: Although money can change a person. It still can't fix a burden. Times is different it isn't our faults money simply talks. It's the easy way to get a point across. People get greedy tend to floss. From their image and things they bought. Overall It won't stop the sadness in time brings madness. Its life money can't buy you happiness.

150. The eye of the tiger: The fierce viper hunting tiger. Very fast smart and hunts prey. He waits for the right move waiting for what he has to do eat. He's marvelous as he creeps, gets very little sleep. Hunting anything to all hoping not to fall. It's his empire his time will soon expire. Deep inside lies fire. Do you see the eye of the tiger?

151. The lighting that struck at midnight: The clock ticked the living time as we exist. What will we commit? As time provokes a flight soon the lighting will strike without a fight. What time maybe midnight? As the time stops you realize of life what you got. Everyone freezes but look in front of you what you got? Your tied like a not nothing but fright at the clear moonlight. That's the lighting that struck at midnight.

152. Do you see what I see: open your eyes and realize what life really is? From a baby to a kid how you are now and where you live. It's not about the past what we did as we now exist. I see forward and predict? My only wish as it begins I hope the world doesn't end. I haven't seen it all so I know I'm missing much. Just trust life's too short I must rush and discuss to all of you. Do you see what you can gain? What you can lose? The decision you choose reflects on how you can improve. What you do see may have you confused. Just fools having fun to amuse and once that's done what do they conclude? You see we are the home of the brave the land of the free. Our fantasies are you and me being anything. With each path comes competition. Life's the ocean were the bait and every day remain fishing. It's the life we all face still racism and judged upon are race just a disgrace. How could this be? Living is not easy you're trying to be you and I'm destined to be me. There're so many close doors and not enough keys to open opportunities upon our world and community. Most people don't live past their teens. There dying in the streets. Man, how could this be happening to us? Now do you see what I see?

153. Life is what you make it: Life is what you make it. Even though our lives are constantly taken. We can't seem to cherish it but have mistaken. It's how you use your voice and be smart with every choice. There're a lot of lanes we don't know on this bumpy road. Life is gold and hard to let go. It's easy to lose control but success brings anticipation. So life is what you make it.

154. Déjà vu: More than a simple dream and flashback it's more back but were looking past that. It's like it happens all over again things fall perfectly in order it begins. You see the same people that were around. You know what's coming making no sound. Things go like before it's like you open a closed door that you saw once more. You want to believe or don't know what to do. It's true you revisited a memory déjà vu.

155. The sunlight that brings out the rainbow: A beautiful day nice weather seems all polite. Do you see this marvelous site? Walk outside and just glare at what's right there. The clouds the sun nothing to fright then comes this precious light and colors appear. I'm standing close and near I can't believe what I see here. Its image I can't let go oh, thanks to sunlight that brings out the rainbow.

156. Kids these days: If you look at the younger generation you would probably shake your head and walk away kids these days in high school doing drugs, sagging their pants, going to school failing their classes, committing crimes, and in gangs what a shame. It seems that parents are not hard enough on their children although kids are sneaky you have kids young having unprotected sex getting girls pregnant and catching diseases. This is not the way for humanity I look at the world in my eyes and see things can be better. Kids don't understand they are born on this earth for a purpose and have their own destiny but the reality they live in is make believe. We need to come together and pray for kids these days.

157. We can change: Sometimes we are characterized as people only the same but I know we can change. We can stop the pain of others we can cherish life value our family tree fathers and mothers. Many people live their life in a false reality thinking it best to be me. This leads to a ego filled with negativity I do believe it's better to be humble it takes struggles to not crumble. Your life is important you mean a lot you are somebody life is what you make it so each choice may it be for a good cause. What is the point of committing crimes? Living in a prisoner society becoming a menace to society it's better if we learn to read create a career a path to guarantee things will be for you and me. To those who have children it's not about you any more life in your hands the plan is to expand and help them get the upper hand. People are having so many kids but it shouldn't be many accidents. A birth shall be planned and understand don't tell a woman you want a baby then leave. Nothing is more import than family! A father must be there for his seed a mother which has barred shall share her love rightfully. So many people hold no beliefs and doesn't see what I see. Too many young black man are lazy and come out to be what society labels them. We can do anything just believe stay consistent to achieve life isn't a game we all have a lane but I know we can change.

158. Hello world: Hello world grown-ups teenagers and kids. I want you to all to know we got to stay focus have faith and keep hoping. Life is not a game no time to be joking. We are only going to be here for a moment, so the dreams you want to receive you have to own it. My message to you is to watch what you do there's a consequence for every single move. Good or bad please enjoy the life you have. Good times won't last smiles and laughs. Don't regret mistakes in the past life's goes by too fast. So to the man understand you have to know no one can do what you can. Treat these women right make that a way of life. To the women make smart decisions don't get hooked on sexual feelings save it for marriage one in a million. Look for the right man no one can go through pain like you can. I dedicate this to every girl and boy in this world and I just want to say hello world.

159.   Trust: It's hard to discuss something like trust. Trust is important to every girl and guy. It's more than you can rely and the truth of why time constantly flies by for you and me. Over time, you will trust many it's more than a connection of your selection. It turns a frown into a smile. People change and keeping it real can be hard to maintain. Things don't always be the same life gets rushed of such and such. Over time, you experience enough but don't give up on God. For you can no matter what always trust.

160.   Follow your dreams: No Matter what people tell you, over anything always follow your dreams. Never give up no matter what give it your all 100% Is not enough. Because life is rough but we must fight for our rights of what we dream to have every night. It's nothing wrong Give it your all everything in your bones. Don't worry you're not alone and the pressure hasn't gone. Even when you retain you don't know what you're going to lose and gain. It begins not the same we all want to be and do that one special thing so keep chasing and follow your dreams.

161.   Air: Something we all share and can't live without here is air. The majority of the earth is composed of oxygen. The trees and plants help produce most oxygen. The way we live the air in life consist, to give a breath of air to give. It's lite as a feather the wind blows showing the weather is there is, just air.

162.   The ladder of life: Each step up takes time. As you go through more you climb. Each step up defines being closer to your path. As time gives signs, we start off on this ladder depending on class. Wealthy, rich, middle, and poor. As we tour looking out there for more. The class defines what you can afford. That doesn't mean you can't find a way to change and climb? Where you are, the position you see. That ladder holds competition. The main goal is to get to the top. Where fame and money is all you got the number one spot. The spotlight means you've done things in your life right. When you're down it's hard to get up you have to start over regain things won't be the same. Where you remain Depends on you and the things you do. But being up high as a kite the top of your life through it all it's the ladder of life.

163.   As I sit and stare: As I sit and stare I see what's really there. I then compare what's not fair reality hits. There is no genie to grant any wish. Perfection we all miss just lurking for God as I exist. I can't see past me every night that I dream. I'm stuck in between what isn't what it seems like the girl of my dreams, my queen, my family tree, my team, or the Devil after me. But I don't scream he can't intervene me living here. I think of so much as I sit and stare.

164. Blame: When you go through things pain rains not feeling the same. Something has changed, you then blame a name or find a person place or time. This kind consists with your sign. Then you see it's all game that's what explains when you blame.

165. Relax: Sit calm what you give, gives back so relax. You don't got to front, act, subtract, and attract. It's a Fact that misery and stress stacks. From nervous breakdowns to collapse. God will have your back get you back, so relax.

166. The wrath of one's fury: Rage can bloom in a hurry. For the wrath of one's fury is unpredictable like a trials jury. This person can penetrate cause more than a hurting. In your soul, you start to lose control such a burden. The eyes can foretell but the action is a surprise. For the wrath of one's fury can be the end of your demise!

167. The tree of generations: Over a billion of branches attached to one gigantic tree. Each branch leads evidentially to you and me. From ages of different races and pages of kids being valued, treasured. The bloodline connects to our ancestors of collectors. From starting with Adam and Eve. The evolution and history which represents every human being, our king. Which brings motivation for each branch of life through the great tree receiving dedication. The life of the tree of generations.

168. Revisit the past: Although time moves forward and the past we can't revisit that. If I could go back there would be a lot of things I would subtract. Not necessarily my mistakes but a new path I would take. Being who I am, I can't escape. As I put my life on a brake and God's word I take. I wish I could go back and redo things. That hurt me still today. Even though it has passed the stress hasn't gone away. Every single day life is a blessing but stay in the present and react to true life facts. Sometimes I have flashbacks thinking how I would change that? If only I could go back. Dear lord, I wish I could revisit the past.

169. Slavery and segregation: From the early 1600's to late 1800's. We as black people were outcast segregated and not treated equally. Through decades of constantly experiencing being degraded, hated for doing nothing wrong. Prejudice towards are skin tone, beaten killed and no remorse. They feel as slaves search for ways to break this cursed. Forced in fields to work, antagonize, and no ways to strategize. Not a planted seed would set them free. I still can't believe what happen to all of thee. Who lived in God's hands but lead to slavery? Separated from others to color pure humiliation. Just the history they suffered through slavery and segregation.

170. The world is going to end: I remember in two thousand twelve the world was predicted to end but failed. Only time did tell that the end is not near. I'm sincere we won't last long here I feel the end is near. It has come clear it's begging. Don't you see my friends the end is planned? I now understand that no matter what I do and who I am won't save what's ahead. It's not just a nightmare I've dreamed in my bed. "I'm going to come for you all" is what the Devil said. The end will come the man you fear will appear and God will be here. "I will have my army and you are his too weak so you won't live mercy I will not give. Once this happens there are no more ways to reinstate your fate but in can change according to judgment day. You will know your way then the new life begins. It's an equinox vision I picture with you because the world is going to end.

171. Life in my eyes: Life in my eyes hit's me with surprise. I realize that things come up like a sunrise. I then decide to recognize what lies in the middle of it all. I then saw something different something I been missing. The sun waves send out a trade I then listen. As the sun glares and glistens what I see right in front of me is true beauty. But the heat represents the pain and cruelty happening upon our community. At the age of 21 there's still a road ahead that's awaiting. For me and God, have several conversations. Then comes the full moon it then glares as I stare and beware, what's out there and after me. I then receive what can lead. As I sit and see jealousy upon poverty. It probably isn't what I actually see and realize. So there're millions of ways to decide life in my eyes.

172. The eye of the tornado: Spinning twirling millions of winds. When the monstrous tornado begins. It spins very fast and sucks up anything in its path. We can run but not hide because the eye will find where you are even if you climb. It will break every obstacle down making sure you are no longer around. It may hit you by surprise. As you get stuck inside and see the place not met for you and me. How can't I escape the eye of the tornado?

173. The gate of fate: Here lies 2 lines which define the path for you and I. Unfortunately, you cannot decide for the answer lies ahead. There're trillions of people standing in these lines. Waiting to find what's about to hit them by surprise. Some already know their fate for a good connection with God that have already made. Some by the Devil played asking to get away. From within the times, they have sinned. It then begins one person after another hoping, in the end, you will see each other. They tell you why in this line you have been kept and left for eternity. The place set for you and me as we stand and wait. To walk through the gate of fate.

174. Marriage: A lifelong commitment to your king or queen. Inherited from God to a ring. You have reached true love and won't hold nothing above. Feelings are at its peak and through this time together anything can be reached. You connect without even speaking. Just pure glare and blinking. One in the mind in time you will find a start. Hopefully, never fall apart you have the key to that person's heart. Being married is a privilege and a blessing pushing towards obsession. Temptations when reached you hate separation. That ring those values show's dedication. Let the path take on its road a never ending show. Together you glow that's when you know you can't let go. You are no longer by yourself but with that person never embarrassed. Soon planning babies in a carriage. A gift to this world you inherit. It's no fairy tale but a blessing by God, it's a marriage.

175.   Procrastination: Saying but not doing sitting but not moving. Thinking but not perusing. Wishing but not getting accepting but not winning. Fantasizing but not realizing just something that brakes us down. Holding us back to wrongful motivation. Which separates us from the success placement. Hurting us all procrastination.

176.   A lie: A lie is a sin and begins false. The cause dissolves after all. We lie to get by life for reasons we don't know why. The habit then multiplies. As we decide to lie not being real. Over time, the truth will reveal but in our souls we kill. It's a lie when your heart pumps and you feel rushed you hush and realize a consequence will hit. Then karma deprives it something that's hurting you and I, a lie.

177.   I had a dream: As like Martin Luther King (Jr) I too one day had a dream. I had a dream that there would be peace on every single corner of the streets. No more prejudice towards our race no more hate and we all were forgiven and given a clean slate. I had a dream that I would publish life in my eyes and it would be bought by every girl and guy. I've been in situations and wondered why so fast the time passes by? I had a dream that everyone would get another chance. God would come to Earth and be our helping hand Sucking all the evil in. I had a dream that another big war would begin and soon the world would end. But let that be done a better way. For I dream when we stand In front of God face to face. On judgment day soon would come our fates? We would be one happy team. Not worried about anything hailing to our king. The visions I've seen in between reality and fantasies. I then prayed to God before I went to sleep. Then the truth all hit and I had a dream.

178.   Hell: Down below where you will rot in eternal flames. For you have failed this game. A damn shame no longer can explain. Look where you remain? Doesn't feel the same. You'd be impressed as you burn in Hell all your flesh. As you see the Devil laughing at your pain and amusement he will gain. He lurks search to hurt you leaving in a stage of not knowing what to do. Listen closer do you hear the flames? It's over no longer on Earth a goner. How can you prevail? For the Devil, your soul has sold. Didn't listen to the right advice people told you. Now you cannot bail but burn so welcome to hell.

179. Water: H20, is water human beings are made of about 60% of water. We have to drink a good percent of water every single day to stay healthy and hydrated. Water comes from everywhere on the earth the oceans, the beaches, ponds, mountains, and wales. Animals drink water insects live in water. Water is a habitat for so many things it helps are bodies get clean.

180. The holocaust: Over 6 million Jewish people at a time of a crisis suffered so much pain and deaths. In Hell is where Hitler is kept. He thought it was right to take away others rights. Then take away many lives. Some did survive but every day I wonder why we didn't stand and fight. You see Hitler was smart and strong build his own army and did nothing but wrong. Jewish people were mistreated outcast and beaten. They were sent to concentration camps killed thrown in damps, prisoners forced to work left dead deserted no help no savior. No one cared treated them like slavery unfair, scared, and beware. They could end up anywhere. Thinking how could this be reality? How could they be separated from their family? Barely fed forced to sleep on unfit beds. This all lead, where was hope and faith to the flag we pledge? Nothing but people abused no rights nothing could help not even the constitution. Thinking back to centuries of many and plenty we lost. Through the worst time ever in history brought, the holocaust.

181. All made equal: We all are one big, family billions of planted seeds can't you see? We are all made equal yes indeed. Once we break off that tree and leaves we want many things. We begin not seeing what we need but greed hoping to succeed. You and I are the same different names and other things between. We're all human beings as I seen other taking life for granted. Mad over their image and because they're not like the others that are winning. Our decisions reflect on us as we proceed to ignore what we see. Where do we lead? We all have a journey waiting ahead. We can't see if it's a bumpy or a steep road. The future we don't know but what matters is who we are what we represent why we are here the sequel. Most of all we are all blessed people and all made equal!

182. The truth will set you free: It seems easy for many to lie and realize we sin. As we begin a curse starting to grow. Once it gets a hold of your soul you will then know it's hard to let go. It's easy to lose control. In time things will connect the truth will progress. As we guess it's over and done then stand in the mirror and look what we become. Something's different in my heart I feel an eternal disease. How could I stop me from where I am and will be? As I believe it will all come out and bleed the poison will leave. I then feel at ease because the truth will set you free!

183. A man with a cold heart: A man with a cold heart, doesn't care, see what's fair, not willing to spare, beware consequences, morally optimistic, selfish, no memory of things they have dealt, with just a bad fish, and luck they have missed. The only wish is to change be forgiven cleanse the spirit to not fall apart. Just hard to start, as a man with a cold heart.

184. Fractals: Almost every handmade thing and nature's creations are shaped of fractals. Think of the structure of leaves the repetitive form it is flowers, trees, T.V.'s, checker boards, and almost every shape created an ever ending shape. Fractals is important in construction it is mathematics and homes are composed of fractals. People don't necessarily see the reality of fractals there are in lungs, kidneys, blood vessels, clouds, and inside the human body. One of the most superior forms is fractals.

185. IF only you could feel what I want you to feel: Feeling's hide body language sometimes lie. What lies deep inside, which runs to the mind? As I decide to give things a try. I feel some type of way I wish I could show you exactly why, for you to understand the man I am is the plan. What I am capable of and to you how I love. Maybe but Heaven's above Maybe, not judge. Get in your comfort zone, talk about such and such your flaws the Skelton's in the closet and all. But trust you, be real to me I'll be real. I just wish you now the deal. I wonder how you would react. If only you could feel, what I want you to feel.

186. The stars that glow at night: Look outside at night and see the beautiful site. Do you see the stars that glow at night? Oh, how they shine so bright and to the sky provides light. They lay higher than a kite. So many stars located far and wide. Each shaped different don't you wonder why they all are differently named, and framed? All-stars but not the same. If you look outside and see something shining bright. It's the stars that glow at night.

187. Things come and go: Sometimes it's okay to let go. Because nothing seems ever final. It's time for you all to know things will always come and go like rain and snow. The sun that glows a sunrise and a rainbow. Throughout life you will have many chances for most will go. When the time comes it will call things small things tall it all in time reloads. Just so you know a lot of things come and go.

188. The message hidden behind: Sometimes even when we read between lines. We still can't find what lies and how to deprive. We take another try to decide and realize sometimes it hides. We cannot grasp it as it passes. Maybe we overlook it too fast. But if you wait and see with your heart and mind. In time, you will find the messages hidden behind.

189.   Life after death: Is there such thing as resurrect? To earn God's full respect someday in his home kept. I've always imagined life after death a complete reset. Let things be reached and met. As I think and prospect how this all would connect? My soul, I hold the Devil won't intercept. Placed in a mind state excavating like crime rate. I close my eyes and see God's gate standing next to me my mate as a sealed fate. My worries and pain cast away. Finally, I pray someday I shall not have left and God I have met in life after death.

190.   When it rains: When it rains the air is thick and cold. When it rains the flowers and plants grow. Just go outdoor when it rains it pours. One drop after another it stops then comes more. The sound of the rain we can't ignore. Growth and life get restored rain, rain wash away the pain. I'm glad you've come ever since I haven't felt the same. For we love when it rains.

191.   Police brutality: Police is represented to protect and serve keeping the world relieved from many crimes. Now on the news you see police brutality as in before when slavery occurred. All police are not the some there are good cops who actually make a good career and done a lot in their time. Then you got crooked cops, harassing people caught on camera beating people. There are races cops, there are professional cops giving all they got but this brutality has to stop. We are all supposed to be equal but some people are judgmental and evil hurting the people, you and me this needs to stop abolish police brutality.

192.   A death left my heart: A death left my heart. That's when all the pain starts I pick up the piece left still falling apart, because a little light left. Now all I see is dark empty feeling symphony, especially when you're more than a friend to me. I'm just reminiscing looking back because the fact I felt love in all my flashbacks. I'm in the present but can't get past that. Even though you are doing better I can't help but love and miss you forever. You I treasure, however for eternity keep your eye close. Make sure I don't fall apart. You're kept in my memories. As a death left my heart.

193.   The pieces of the puzzle: It seems all subtle for the pieces of the puzzle aren't fully connected it is God choice to resurrect it. It's he who protects it. As life is such a blessing these pieces are addressing. To become reality but a blind naked eye can't see what is meant to be. Getting on track, in fact, seems make believe. The day this fully connects eaven you shall fully see. They're pieces planted by the Devil to deceive. The truth of the matter something complete is not always received. Try taking apart your soul something only God can see. This is meant only spiritually. May the angels keep others out of trouble? The Devil and his demons are in a huddle. For it is angels and demons which will rumble. A time before mankind. As we are blind to the pieces of the puzzle.

194. A man's lost is another man's treasure: A man's lost is another man's treasure however that other guy might treat her better. Love is pain, pain is pleasure. Good things don't last forever. So be careful how you choose and be clever. Sometimes women rain like the weather usually, women change after a relationship from the trust the style to smile. Because in the past what they dealt with. A lot of dudes get jealous because you got a new man and it got all together. So don't forget a man's lost is another man's treasure.

195. A soldier: A man that fights till it's over never fear's death. Even though you know it's getting closer. Through it, all the pain going insane. You still remain holding your composer. A rare breed a four leaf clover. A real man a soldier.

196. My brothers: We all hold pride you and I resemble a guy. We multiply through planted seeds you and me. I do believe we represent half of humanity. Is this how it's planned to be? All I see is close friends and others. Truth be told you all are my brothers.

197. When will we learn: When will we learn that there's consequence for every choice you make? When will we learn that it will be our turn to make our own fate? With God's aid he will show us the way through Heaven's gates. When will we learn that out there isn't safe? Constantly judge and overlook on our race. When will we stand together for the better and cherish God forever? When will we make choices clever? As the time passes the sun burns and each joyful day we earn. To live it all right when will we learn?

198. Let the sunrise clear the rain: Let the sunshine clear the rain, wash away all the pain. As another beautiful day, we gain let there be change. May the sunrise shine and clean out our insides. Let the rain, at first, baptize each heart that cries. Let the sunshine change the dark as the light start help us stay from falling apart. As the rain drops before joyful tears crying out for more. Each drops the world it explores as it washes away every sin. Then God forgave every women and man. The Devil hailed but then God came. As he let the sunshine clear the rain.

199. Let go my fears: It's hard to let go my fears. As I see the world unclear I don't feel safe here. Even though I know God is near. I still swift in life as I steer. I'm driving, denying, and running from the past. I see the Devil behind me coming fast. I then step my foot on the gas and accelerate at full blast. How long will it last? In a flash, more pain will pass. I close my eyes and let go and God then controls and appears. As death comes near. I ask for forgiveness as I let go my fears.

200.   My mind says one thing but my heart says another: My mind says one thing but my heart says another. If I guess I won't always recover the best. I'm stressed because my mind's thinking this but my heart won't let. The meaning of it all I protect. The real answer and choice I strive to collect. I think about such and such. What do I trust? I can't give into my mind in time just rush. My heart beats I listen and hush but words don't flow. So how will I know how to discuss but still I haven't let go and given up. Soon everything will come together as one. The answer I will recover still mind says one thing but my heart says another.

201.   The sculpture tatted in my heart: I pledge of allegiance to God to give all my heart and soul. Wash away my sins as I begin with you until the end. Let light guide me through and one day see you. I let down my guard fully and pray you get fully through me. Tell me what I'm here for? Who I am as I earn the reward to be allowed in your open door. Entering the space the pain will erase. As I feel at ease with your grace. I thank you for bringing me to this place. For an eternity blessing to start. Together we will never fall apart. I write down the sculpture tatted in my heart.

202.   Have mercy on my soul: I'm not perfect but a growing men. I know at times I sin, but as this journey moves on reality begins. I foresight my future to the end. Just hoping I will win. It's hard following every 10 commandments and understanding why these Godly rules are so important. Because without world distortion proportion of human follow and God love they shall swallow. It doesn't take today or tomorrow but the time of life we burrow. Let God forgive our sorrows. We all hear about the right things but truth be told we act like we don't know. I just beg forgiveness and may God have mercy on my soul.

203.   The perception of love: The way I perceive love from experiences of all the above. I look upon love as a rainbow it doesn't come true much comes and goes. As I look at this rainbow in my mind. I know there're so many colors but the truth will show. As the sun glows it can end fast can start slow. In time in your heart and soul, it will control. As feelings unload some try to deny but realize love can't hide. No matter what it will find. You then decide to recognize the blessings of God he constantly provides met for you and I. Searching for the right one we can only try. You will find as it seems to hide like pride. It's more than to smile or cry. As I defined physically and mentally what this precious love can be. You see I'm not just speaking for me. All I see is lots of open opportunities. But I will never know what's right for me. When it's time in your mind in your soul and heart will reveal. You take care of that person like a nurse. It begins real when you put that person first. It's hard to believe that someone loves you, at times you may feel used and confused. Thinking why am I the one to choose? What do you want from me? How long will this last? Where will we lead? Dear God please explain to me. It can't be real love but if there's absolutely nothing that can come over or above. Then it must be real, that's how I see the perception of love.

204. The shadow that follows me: Perfectly representing me, I look in the mirror and see who I stand to be. As I walk outside in the dark that's when it starts following, the shadow that follows me. Watching and see in front of what leads. I feel no fear but see I'm here and help is near. As the shadow appears. I know I'm not the one here. I'm sincere the shadow will even wash away my tears. Finally, someone that I can love and won't judge. As it won't leave till the sunlight appears keeping it away from me but I still see the shadow that follows me.

205. Creativity: A blessings in us, as I explain creativity. More than an ability but it really looks to me as being expressive another hidden side inside ourselves. By showing at ease we felt the passion to our own fashion. Just as a more self-satisfaction can lead to many reactions. It's all in us, essentially a living versatility through a positive ego that leads to creativity.

206. Without God: Without God there be no us and trust you and I wouldn't even be able to discuss. Without God no world, no boys, and girls. Without God, no Heaven or Hell and the world you see would fail. If you see that for real there's no hope or no faith each and every day. We couldn't even pray no fate no gate no race. This world wouldn't exist as I think back and predict. It just makes me sick because we are so blessed a lot. There's no history past or future without God.

207. The giving tree: The tree gave air to the boy and together they shared much joy. The tree was the boy's favorite toy. It begin when they were both small and shared multiple memories. As the tree grew tall the boy then saw a change things that weren't the same. Each day the boy came many memories exchanged. The boy had a name for the tree. He said "you seem to give so much to me love, support, air, and show so much care when I was hungry you dropped an apple there and when fear was near gave me beware you see I look upon this Earth and can't be the same as everybody I cherish life because to me you always been the giving tree"

208. Who do you believe in: Those in this place with hope and grace our history of God has given a trace? It must be a reason, so I ask who do you believe in? Is it Buddha, Jesus, God, the sun God, Yama-way, and God's in Greek mythology. May the light shine on thee, my eyes bleed? All I see is a world filled with misery.

Is this how it's supposed to be? God all mighty can you lead me the way? Now may we stand in a circle bow our heads and lets us pray to the one leading the way. Every day I must say it isn't easy to believe but soon destiny will unleash its state in the line of fate. For those who find the key to that locked door furthermore entering Heaven's gate. Our dignity and pride we must separate. Deep inside lies the spirit hidden in us. Those are blind to see the shadow of light following but receive the dark. As they don't believe. How can humanity be so naïve? Maybe in our soul, we will conceive? Maybe in a day? Maybe in a season? So I still ask you all who do you believe in?

209. Imprisoned in the mind: Close your eyes look into the mind for a certain sign. There's a room there but beware you trapped here. The end is near and Satan will appear. As you're sitting in a chair looking out as you stare. Seeing the shape of your fate square. He then declares words of the wise but you're traumatized. You realized how can I survive? If I can't speak out and apologize. You then relax back and recognition there lies a way to escalate and climb. You then find as time moves by your imprisoned in the mind.

210. The secret among society: Emperors rearranging their gracious desire. Will not be legalized feared petrifies. Inspire but acquire wealth using stealth to burn fire. A secret race placed where ever fear can be tasted. Organize fate as it all pasted unknown among and erased. Eyes confirm special conversations predicting equations among our nations. Which reserve separations the world nights despite revealing changed lives spookier than the moonlight. As the future provoke to maintain and ignite people we fright. Unless targeted do bite impossible to see at site. They might invite being polite the decision of a new trial or denial then filed x out and suicidal. You and I know maybe you don't know constantly deciding and the world change they are providing. The merciful illuminate, the secret among society.

211. The grim reaper: The Devil's hit man no one does believe no one can see him or understand. When he shows your life he will conceive. For when it begins the world will end pain will lend the rules will bend. No one can intervene his work no man, he provokes death to unload and possess your soul. Bringing you to the place for eternity that's opposite of cold. When you see him you will know, lose control beg for mercy but he won't let go of your soul. The seeker and keeper the grim reaper.

212. The key to success: In order in life to do things right and progress. From being blessed, you will over time collect the keys to success. As life is a test and you would never guess how things going well can intercept. The concept is to believe and not let things unattainable to be met. This project has requirement to pass and many questions you ask to complete this task. It comes by so fast and our past can't hold us a loser. We measure dreams to obtain super then hits the future. It comes as you become different affiliated with politicians and recognize competition. The key which leads in the sea as we remain fishing our main mission. Good advice of life we must listen. We all strive and wonder why you and I atomized? We realized were simply impressed then we collect the keys to success.

213. Actions speak louder than words: Adjective nouns and verbs are the least concern because actions speak louder than words. It's superb how sticks and stones can break your bones. Words define what's going on it doesn't reveal what's real for how you feel is concealed until the actions let out what's the deal. Words can hurt actions can kill changed by the mind frame appeal. If it's going to happen then comes the moment and the play which is the reaction. The main attraction is more than speaking listening to what you heard. So actions speak louder than words.

214. Looks can be deceiving: Not everything you see you must believe in because looks can be deceiving. The site of your eye you are perceiving can be leading to something different morally optimistic. For looks are falsely consistent. As we are curious, suspicious but behind the lines you will find in your mind that time brings out situations misleading. For looks can be deceiving.

215. A divorce: Separation between you and me as time has played its course. Many people go through a divorce. No longer with love support for feeling have deported, left memories and pain is kept. Although it's finished a broken life commitment. The privilege through God to a ring for him and her king and queen. It seems the Devil has intervened. The time fly's by to keep together you both tried. So you gave up not knowing exactly why. In your heart saying goodbye this is the end for you and me. Please for all I've done I apologize. I know how it feels inside when the ring is no longer on your finger and set aside. No longer in my life you shine. For its forever dark we have torn apart there's no sunrise upon a girl or guy. That decision you decide deprives. No remorse no looking back time has played its course. You get everything together a lawyer and file for a divorce.

216. Eyes do more than see: Although perceiving everyday reality between you and me, we are the rare breed. As more reincarnated planted seeds proceed to lead to every human being. But between us all, everybody can you see the rain heart trouble call? When things are overlooked the reaction that takes differently. From skimming through a book as you see what's right in front of thee. Whatever leads is your eye to conceive and the messages will receive. I do believe eyes do more than see.

217. Jealousy: Jealousy is hate, disgrace and separates in your mind state. As you wait for it to build over days. Jealousy upon race set aside for you take away their pride but evolution will decide. The solution as problems rise what do you decide? To let it go give it a try then, you know that person got to die. That's how it starts between you and me. There hiding all wearing a disguise to deprive. The stats will arrive things will lead. Plain and simple the world is full of jealousy.

218. There's always a way out: When broken down suffering from a drought. Time will tell days will count because there's always a way out. Show no fear hold no doubt. Some way you will figure out. Hope and have faith that maybe soon but maybe not today. For God will shed his grace to any person on this place. Any belief or race it's all timed by pace. The pain will separate soon you will be in a better state. No need to shout hold the pain inside don't pout. No matter what there's always a way out.

219. The fire burning inside: As pain applies between you and I. Heat arrives as the fire is burning inside. Holding pride means not to cry but try to let go and deny. For there's a place to fry but not met for you and I. Usually fire is started from wood rubbing together doing no good. Then the flame begins the fires is understood. To put it out in ourselves we wish we could. For us, it starts when we sin. Then the flames reinstate again. How could we not let in? For we are almost made of all water. How could the inside get any hotter? As you sweat tears mercy of God is met, set to protect. The Devil selects to get you away from God and set aside as you reframe petrified. Then lies the fire burning inside.

220. 9 lives to live: I believe like a cat we have 9 lives to live. From human to pet animals and insects. I believe when you die we get resurrected and our souls are kept. What changes is the flesh as you leave to Heaven or ell still are soul can sell. Another life will prevail maybe you can't tell. Someone close is living with you right now. For a new life, they have found. Watching over you but cannot provide a clue for you must conclude. The path which is given to me I hope the message will receive. People dead still exist because we all have 9 lives to live.

221. Humanity: Human beings I mean everything boys and girls kings and queens. We all through history and every single planted seed represents "humanity" It impresses me especially when so many haven't seen what lies in my eyes as I see. Why you and I constantly being born and die? But there's a plan set aside for you and I. Present past and future represent the last each person life ends so fast. So I then ask you all who exactly are we? More than human beings blessed on God's team. Rightfully on this planted 100% of humanity.

222.   The circle of the sun: I dedicate this to my old school SCPA, from 6-12 grad. Every day I look upon where I am from and what I know I've become in the circle of the sun. As the sun waves hit heat consist as each individual creative soul at SCPA exist soon to graduate gone in the mist. As life twist we all known never to quit words I can't don't apply why because you and I will soon rise like the sun. Throughout life becoming a great one from the teachers and believer's critics and perceivers are daily procedures learning leadership gain trust and relationship experiencing everything where delt with but in that circle and on stage lies each person in a gifted stage. See how SCPA students can amaze have your mind in a daze. As they burn fire and hold parades dancing acting singing writing exercising learn to fight but use for surviving. The home of the most fun SCPA the circle of the sun.

223.   Moving mountains: As I visit the holy waters in Heaven I see a special falcon right next to a secret place with moving mountains. Inside the mountains lie holy water to baptize all people who become an angel. In Heaven the journey to get there as far away I saw and stared. There was a forest in front. To get through the Angel of the forest would have to give you approval, Mother Nature. As I prance through the forest as a temporally tourist. Finally I reach my destination but approach with Hesitation. I felt nothing but sensation as I arrived I saw the falcon which crosses my eyes. He was drinking water from the mountain fountains. It seems on this day all sins I washed away I closed my eyes and prayed. As the water touch my flesh the pain finally left a halo was kept. A better life accounting thanks to Jesus Christ I saw the light, it was hidden in the moving mountains.

224.   Behind closed blinds: Behind closed blinds, you will find unknown sings. The enemy lines people who commit crimes, make a choice with no remorse and the Devil will support. As they burn their soul without a torch. For time is playing its course. The cops try to stop, report, and support. The mind changes over time. Soon you will find what's hidden behind closed blinds.

225.   God works in mysterious ways: From looking upon us every day listening to each soul as they pray. I must say God works in mysterious ways. Everything he has created is for a reason. From holidays, seasons, morning, and evenings. To each human being right now breathing. I've always wonder especially today how is it possible that every person place or thing God regulates? Why did it all begin? Why did God die on the cross for all our sins? Why is a woman created for a man? There is so much I can't even understand. When I think of the Lord he is more than a friend. How is it that there is no obstacle? You complete miracles doing the impossible. Everything is for a purpose and God is merciful. Planning things every single day. God works in mysterious ways.

226. This Christmas: This day I woke up and prayed. A Christmas day without presents still my Christmas spirit has not cased away. I'm no longer a boy I'm grateful for love, not presents and toys. I'm thankful to be alive. I remember staying up until Christmas day to open presents. Although a gift is a blessing without many I see a better message. I've realized this is the birth of Jesus a day to love receive and give. I never believed in Santa clause, this wasn't my fault. Young I was taught the presents under the tree my parent's family and friends had bought. It doesn't matter how much it cost. What matters is the expression. I guess Christmas can break depression it comes once a year. In the eye of children Santa clause appears riding through town with a sleigh and his rain Deer's. Under the chimney, he drops down looking to see if his cookies and milk are around. He has written a world list, rather naughty or nice. The nice receive something children would believe. For me it seems the Grinch has taken the presents away. I only need God's love on this Christmas day!

227. Out of my mind: I found a way out of my Mind. Out of my heart Out of my soul. At that moment, I Tread the sea, the shores which breezed it departed me separately. My mind is but a room So much information Consumed, This abyss is my tomb. A mind is a terrible thing to Waste that would be my doom! There are connections in Me As I am a battery, Sending's signs to further me. I take out negativity Endure positivity to be sure I'll Furthermore my Capabilities. I have a sense of humor my hostility is my ego's Consumer. My thoughts which conflict Faults Have stricken a tumor. A mind is a terrible Thing to waste. How can I fill my memory a hard drive with So much space? My heart is but a vase my soul which is divine It seems connectivity would Trace. I fought my way past my expectations. No hesitation I Would tread the sea the wave of me Morally the Advisory Opposing my measures. I'm happy for progression, but always can do better. They say a wise man is Clever and knowledge is forever. Power is knowledge the more you know the More you don't know. But I for one can be slow I can miss the bigger picture the just of it won't always Show. I'll pray today as tomorrow let God on my soul take full Control. I hope he will bind send out a special sign. The moment we become fully divine. I would journey to a new path and at last Out of my mind!

228. The clouds: Circle shaped and escape the late holding a smile watching all who's down. The clouds representing the weather blocking part of the sun for the better. The site we all see together until the end forever. Some big some small but as you seen the clouds won't fall. Some days we realize it rains, they cry wondering why drops will fall and rain will fly. As it begins the clouds washing all our sins moving light as the wind. Making no sound in the day always around, the clouds.

229.   Mind over matter: Look into your mind freeze time. Look in the mirror reality hits them everything comes clearer. Man in the mirror not taking over my spirituality. My mind frame is allergic to pain like allergies. I hold account my ego above the balcony. Then hits a mystery people trying to hold you down its jealousy. You can't hurt me God keeps me company. Faith will make a way pull me away like a rope holding on to pride then hits hope. I contain myself hold my composer like a Blatter. It's all a hit and I'm the batter. I hit a home run for the fear has scattered. To overcome anything it takes mind over matter.

230.   Cause and effect: Each choice you make has a consequence and karma hit's time is left. Given in cause and effect. The move you make as you select. Soon the result will be kept. Rather its obsession causing depression each lesson is a blessing. What is taught the message brought is a weapon? In school young and pursued things dumb. I look back to what I have become reflecting where I am from. This is to everybody I'm not the only one. But obligating prior to motivations because separation the near placement of what we are facing. The unknown is erasing so let each choice bet be your best decision. We all know there's are a cause and effect.

231.   Let there be: Let there be sunshine. Let there be rain let there be many blessing to gain. Let there be no more pain. Throughout the things that exchange, let God reclaim that we are all equal all the same. Let the light reveal if God's real. Let there be a miracle changing our souls. Let it be cold as we stand froze every bit of stress we let go. All I see is you and me In God we must trust and believe. We will receive what's ahead to see, so let there be.

232.   The Government: Society has a political organizing system we see them as the government. Think of the tree of life but reflected through our liberty. The house of Congress senates, the Supreme Court, lower courts, representatives, the electrical college. This congregation institutes plans the upper hand people don't understand politics. We live in a world of laws and amendment as people vote as Candidates run in an election to become President. Our country has suffered through a depression as history recession. Life in my eyes is my most obsession. People are liberal freedom is what America defines the land of the free we have democratic candidates and people the democracy of a sequel. Decide what's best through laws passed as the president protects the congress either accept or neglects. We have republicans to seek to regulate inflation multiply money keeping things running. Civilization can see life in a regular reality there are high power versatile human beings seeing life in a 3d picture. I look upon classified society wealthy, rich, middle class, to poor people outdoor. We are a nation structured by higher demands as a human being I feel big, alive but an audience to the stage, the government.

233. Copper sun (inspired by the book cooper sun): At a point and time I find even at home it is enemy lines. They took us all, I knew when I saw it happened, in the end, I would fall. We all got broken apart how could people be this cruel. Do they have a heart? It was back then slavery had started. We lived in a village and now I see freedom is a privilege. Throughout my journey looking back at where I am from. I see what I now become a slave filled with rage stuck in a maze caught in a daze. As the sun waves blazes for days I pray for ways to escape. It's hard for women with certain religion seeing what's giving. Just to smile or how a good feeling. I look at my chances getting out one in a million. As things remain I hold no doubt but cannot shout. For me to be free make a way I must figure out. When the sun is up I feel down because my family is no longer around. When the sun is out in the dark starts I still hold pain my heart. My chances of getting out are like flipping a copper dime. Heads or tail? Only time will tell if I fail. My soul will sail as I run in the copper sun.

234. As a young black man: People just don't understand it's hard being viewed by society as a young black man. Anything you want to achieve, believe we can. It isn't easy for most of us still aren't free. Can't you see you and me have to do better for our community? Once you are 18 viewed as an adult. Some quick to fight for the most, constantly pulling the rope. From boy to men grown too old. Truth be told we will never hold the upper hand. It's hard as a black man.

235. When the stars shine: Look at the sky at night and see what you will find. Don't you see the twinkle little stars shine? There is no sun to provide light. This makes me wonder in fright? But still hold excite I wonder if the truth will be bright? The stars will ignite. How can I see you but you are so far? I wonder where you are you shining stars. It's bizarre how the sky has stars and somehow from up above giving off light while the sun is hiding behind. Isn't that the reason why when the stars shine?

236. The scars in life: I never would guess I have scared my flesh. Seems the scars in life God has request? They say a fresh wound has consumed pain all left for a scar to gain. From a cut on your body and a cut to your heart. A piece has been torn apart it then starts to bleed. Now we have received a likely disease. As thought by an attack of an enemy. Then you see what has been cut. You put a bandage on after, cleaning the scar. You're filled with rage then hits a stage in a page of a maze. The scar leaves the cut has hidden away. The image provokes you to excite. Just days of a prisoner to the scars in life.

237. You look I look: She appears as if beauty is there. We then share a moment to dare. You glance I stare, I'm shook you look, I look. Somehow in my heart I start by not judging a cover by its book. I analyze and realize the back of the cover. Compatible enough to be my lover. Seems like no other, hides the natural beauty undercover. She seems sweet as a mother. Shock inside, we both begin with simple words to apply. You're a girl and I a guy. We both try to put the past aside. For a moment and let the moment play. In my mind, I find a sign with creative words to say. You listen and feel amazed. I'm staring at your beautiful face and hallucinate being with your every single day. At the same time in my head in my head, I pray. He speaks to me as you talk, I wait. It seems my wish he has granted and took. I open my eyes bout to cry feeling good inside. You look I look.

238. Everyone gets forgiven: A message to all men and women, I know you make the wrong choices and bad decisions. But, by God, everyone gets forgiven. For each soul today living. I let you know that the road is filled with dark but the light will glow. The right way to live will show and each state will be clean the pain will explode. You're forgiven, let go. Let the change exchange help out my frames. Let grace rain our soul is driven. Have mercy on our souls, for everyone gets forgiven.

239. The future: The picture has been closely painted. Excavating foresight far as a consultation. Our world our nation the future is awaiting. I predict it in a more spiritual conversation. For ahead holds many reservations. Today and now brings motivation. For soon will be different separations. Our President bringing dedication from the history of tracing. Now in the time of this placement the life we are facing. The past we are erasing. In coming soon, the time is here. Some will experience it lot's will disappear. It will be here, the future.

240. Under the mistletoe: Under the mistletoe, a connection starts to grow. Somehow the mistletoe takes somewhat of control. The kiss that comes will show. This precious moment we can't let go. As love is hidden wrapped in a bow. Soon it will consume like the cold and snow. Then you will know, how it feels under the mistletoe.

241. Sharing is caring: A good heart is comparing and sparing. The world would be a better place sharing is caring. For a second helping someone else instead of yourself, in the end, how would you have felt? A good choice is dealt and selfishness will soon melt. As life tightens on you like a belt. Care will be appearing sharing is caring.

242. Can: A look can break a closed-door. A conversation can lead to more A good man can change a broken heart and God can keep us from falling apart.

Just a glance and things can start. The right women can touch your heart. A smile can take away the pain and as things exchange love will gain. If it's too hot soon it will rain. Don't lose hope and take the lord in vain. A situation can change your frame. A mother can give you a name. Déjà vu means in the same. A bible can cure a soul. Truth be told life impacted by God can be gold.

243. Stay in your own lane: Follow your road stay in your own lane. In this world, we are blessed to have come. Given a name all made equal but not the same. I see life as a journey four lanes different beliefs. There's no telling when entering this path what will reach? I am sure you all heard by now of the fast lane? Where things change you live life like soon it's going to end. Taking sins for a spin soon it will begin. Then there's a regular middle lane. Where we start a moderate lifestyle we gain. It's more of accepting your flaws begging for forgiveness. Things which lead to more shy, timid, and right beside is the slow lane. You are scared and beware have fears what's hidden there. For a lot is in stored but to your eye disappear. Picture you as a car moving on this freeway in your own lane. Each one something different you will gain. There's laws particular the speed limit. You can't finish if you don't obey. You see to eyes of society we are prey. Hundred's every day it's simply what you can handle. From a car automatic or manual things come to scandals. The crowd won't burrow God's mercy and grace. To anticipate past those sorrows how you live today impacts tomorrow. Just so you know follow your own road of live. To do things right and obtain gold. You see things aren't the same, so stay in your own lane.

244. Living the dream: Mirror, mirror on the wall. I see the past the things that went good and fall. I know that one day god will call, and explain to me why I went through it all. Me under his wing he is my father my king. Living the dream on his team nothing outside of his spirit will intervene. He knows my past my present and future that withholds. Trusts his words the bible and stories told. My journey lies here on Earth, he has been there through my heart. His spirit and love gave me birth. I am to learn him, worship him, and show what he is worth. Every day from that faithful day that I chose to give in to him every single way. I shall listen understand and obey. Love him follow his spirit touch and pray. Asking for forgiveness of my mistakes. I will give all my heart. He is why I'm blessed to be here from the start. That day is when you are saved reborn loved for a new beginning and start. Live through God, and he won't fail u or let u fall apart. When you leave and die to him you will fly. Be in his home and greatness will redeem. That day u will realize you are living the dream.

245. Bottles of sorrow: Trying to let go the pain. Drinking to forget and change your mind frame. Crying inside but lie fronting to be fine. Imprisoned of the mind, there's a ladder to climb. To grasp that alcohol, beer or bottle of wine. You're stuck on it all the time. Wanting to quit but as your conscious consist the addicting still exist. You set out a plan to stop and predict. There lies in that bottle that you swallow the Devil. Holding on to your soul till tomorrow. The sin you borrow then follows in the bottle of sorrow.

246. God please: God please help me out. Show me what the world's truly about. Each day I pray, I beg you forgive me for my sins and guide me to a better state. I learn we cannot always have it your our way. I wonder to this day why when we talk I can't hear what you say. I give it a moment of silence but hear no sound. I somehow believe and feel you're around. Watching over me right now God, please give me the strength to get up when I down. Bring a smile to my face and wipe away my frown. I wish I never did a lot of things I did. As I still live as a kid in my mind I find I'm losing time. I think back to the past and rewind. Letting go leaving the past behind. I'm steady trying to reach the upper room but can't see a ladder to climb. Things aren't as straight as my spine. I look upon others, friends, my family, brothers, father, and mother. In their soul, I picture a painted picture being painted. Through good times and dark roads that they fainted. Perfection I know we aren't it. I beg and beg for forgiveness as life experiences are my witness. In this world, I have no business. I think why me, not a planted seed? I hold many deeds and so many blessing I have received. When I die you I want to see God, please.

247. Until the end of time: Perception of my solitary mind. The conscious interception blessing that I find. Avoiding sinning and committing crimes. I extol God until the end of time. It's evident written in my lines still feeling fears and beware. Cautious but fatuitous holding no doubt life I flout still searching for everything to figure out. Life changes things are incurable to avoid. I'm so scared to die feeling paranoid not knowing what to do. Lurking for signs but still very little clues the choices that I choose. I pray I learn from my mistakes and hope not to lose The Devil is mendacious simply dividend but impactions you. God told us to be fruitful and multiply set aside our sins and still hold our pride. Deep inside our souls if we don't we will fry. To get sanction by God, in the end, I promise I will do more than try. A message to you and me until the end of time.

248. Rise over run: Just as the sun rose and the day begun, rise over run. The day has started the sun is shining brightly on the Earth bringing light. It seems everything is ok this beautiful day. As I awoke like yesterday I will get on my knees and pray. Asking God for his grace wondering what I am to do on this place. I get up look in the mirror at my face and hope not to get judged and feel disgrace. From then and now history will trace. If it's too much evil God will change this place. As evil can rise soon it will come and run. No more worries none. We all hope in the end to God we will be sent when it's all said and done rise over run.

249. So many babies being born: So many babies are being born. So many wounds are being torn. It seems these seeds exceed planted corn but are morally hard to afford. The reward is the blessing of God sent to Earth. These children we gain many bring change. For each is made equal but not the same. As sisters and brothers consist of Adam and Eve our long existing tree of our father and mother. It starts to form two bringing forth you. I see what these kids turn out to be. You and me so many blessings we have received. Although we are humanity but life brings insanity. Making us blind to see what God wants out of thee. The spirit of God is forever worn and so many babies are born.

250. The dirt in our skins which brings forth sins: In order to clean out our insides we have to be baptized. For you and I extend trends and it begins the dirt in our skin which brings forth sins. As I thread the needle in my skin. Hoping to stop the bleeding the grace of God to live an eternal life in the end. It isn't easy to let go in order to be lead down the right path we have to be forgiven and hope to last. As the time pass and then we ask God to wash away the dirt hiding in ourselves every day. Not even a shower will devour the sins of ours. Not even rain will wash away which lies poisons us every day. As we pray to let go and hope God promotes his holy soul. To those who don't know let us change the filth hidden in. May God extinguish the dirt in our skin which brings forth sins?

251. The fatal disease spreading upon humanity: Generations from history, still from now to you and me. I can see the fatal disease spreading upon humanity. This is something I feel it has to be discussed because it is affecting us. The dollar bill in God we trust has crushed so many lies. I despise and feel the Devil is a lie. Even though it's the only way to survive holding a trade erasing you and me. As God says "walk by faith not by sight" The land of Havilah where gold is found brings forth a site. The disease sucking in evil a parasite. From Gold to now what we hold. Truth be told freezing our souls cold. It isn't our fault dollar bills can talk as it stalks following you and me poisoning everybody. Money the fatal disease spreading upon humanity.

252. Men can be dogs: Throughout my life experiences, as I saw, I see men can be dogs. Wanting sex from women, that's all. This likely disease can make you fall. Why is it that man don't understand that women are more than friends? Together they fully blend you see only body language can pretend but feelings show what's real in the end. It makes me mad to only hear how men leave women pregnant and disappear. Left alone did wrong now that you're gone that baby, you had now she's left to be the dad. This isn't how things should be you and I shall treat women rightfully. I hope God blesses thee soon better life for women to receive. If you believe react, watch, and see the light will appear even in the fog. Most men can be dogs.

253. Treat others how you want to be treated: Treat your neighbor with respect then friendship shall connect. Those who snake seem to get deleted. Each person needs to treat others how you want to be treated. If in yourself you have a heart as relationships start to keep things from falling apart. Being real is how it starts feelings and healing comes out to be revealing. How things proceed to be proceeded the best way to live every day is to treat others how you want to be treated.

254. The dark and light: The dark which is evil and produces cold creatures lurking and unknown the opposite of light a terrible site. The light hope faith which brings heat the time where it isn't easy to creep. The time where most don't sleep the dark represents Satan the light which is God. Both come out once a day both times for each soul to pray. If I shall die before I wake. I hope things come out right in the dark and light.

255. The last of a dying breed: A message to us, every human being from now to every future planted seed. Always hold God over everything and cherish every moment like wedding rings. There's only one God only one king and fully on his team, no one can intervene. It if only means don't let sins come between. I feel the end is near and soon the Devil will appear. Wiping out all humanity here a worst nightmare. Even if war we declare it's not going to be fair. So hold on to God but beware were riding on this road but not alone God shall steer. Only he truly cares for every child barring a smile you got to stand tough. Don't let the Devil hold you down and living right through Christ the Lord shall have found. Nothing but grace all around to every soul more than a million. Soon you will see as a vision I proceed and every person on this earth will leave. Please God, have mercy on thee the last of a dying breed.

256. Truth or dare: Truth is real what God makes us feel. Dare is to sin and begins to beware breaking the commandments not showing care. Dare is to spare what's true there truth is to believe and actions soon will speak. Once revealed you will see you and me dare to make choices as if God's not watching their truth is he always here. Although throughout life both can compare. We all share moments of truth or dare.

257. Be yourself at all times: Be yourself at all times for then you will find signs that lead to the truth hidden behind. In your mind we try to impress but what's left to be you and cherish that you're blessed. With a future as life is a test, it's best to not let a fake image connect. Be you be true watch what you do. No need to be cool or act or a fool commit wrongful crimes. Stay in line with God you will find. Be yourself at all times.

258.   Is this how it's supposed to be: Is this how it's supposed to be you and me no longer allowing our hearts to reach and speak? Don't you think of me at least once a week? Do you think back and peek without me my comfort don't you feel weak? When it's hard and the hill is steep don't you wish I was there to sweep you off your feet? Without me doesn't life feel obsolete, not complete? You don't feel it being real right now. One day you will see. Is this how it's supposed to be robbery and deaths all over the streets? People scared to even sleep. Is this how it's supposed to be the government pursuing to help but destroying us? Hurricanes destroying community, cities, and countries. Who do you believe me or people who turn to be enemies? Are you a friend of me? Why attack, subtract, look back, and wrongfully react. A fact the world is a terrible place judgment upon a face disgrace upon a race. When will it fade away? There needs to be a change today. Something I just can't see, is this how it's supposed to be?

259.   Pray for my downfall: If I could make a phone call to you all. I would simply ask to pray for my downfall. Help me get up and stand tall let me get over my flaws. Cleanse me wash my paws for I have and been through enough. At times, life is rough it's hard to gain strength to stay tough. Pray for me as I pray for you. Let one move change our grooves to God we shall salute. More worthy than the law a message to you all pray for my downfall.

260.   We all are not perfect: A thing that is certain we are all not perfect. As each sin makes us nervous leaving a burden. Its like your heart is skipping a beat for the most not praying before you sleep. Sometimes we must be neat and relax back taking a seat. Soon a mistake will creep it may be deep like pulling a teeth. This is like burning in the heat only holy water can cleanse your soul. Which resonates and then you will know your flaws we can't forever hold. As being bold then being told habits get old. For the most accept that you will fail but always prevail to God your soul you will sell. Only time will tell what reveals but be patient and chill. Change on how you feel. One thing that's for certain we all are not perfect.

261.   Our covenant deeds: To God we can achieve anything and as a blessed planted seed we can soon see and believe the Devil will try to conceive us. To me, life is being honest a faithful promise. Life goes by so fast like sonic morally ironic. So many sins have you hook like a phoenix. We are too blind to foresight beyond It. For every human being, we have unnecessarily needs. It is our covenant deeds that help us exceed through Christ living right. Day after day night after night through belief and battles fights after fights. They're multiple tickets to multiple flights. But which airline will ignite to Heaven's gate sealing are fate? Revealing our soul mate that God has a mate for us to soon date and take. Make no mistake it's never too late for the Lord is forgiving. Even on your decisions through guidance and Christ were rightfully winning. Although sinning makes us usually blind to see you and me. In order to succeed, we have to fully succeed through our covenant deeds.

262.   Each sacrifice pays its price: My message and advice throughout life is things won't always go right but each sacrifice pays its price. Rather it's people to see why we are all equal. Rather it's habits to foresight the sequel. We, the people don't always see the full the picture painted for parts are separated outdated. Through rightful conversations brings a sudden motivation. Dedication after chasing than an occasion the life we are facing through the history of tracing. As time is racing and life is ancient you have to forgive to get give up and commit. What words and signs define ways to better the life of yours and mine? We cannot recline for in time it will be unknown. Rolling a dice might not be something you like but each sacrifice pays its price.

263.   Wealthy promotes most souls unhealthy: Being filthy rich is a disease spreading as you itch. The path and choices you pick consist as you exist. We cannot predict for life can trick being hard as a brick. You're stuck in a wrongful reality like a stick. Soon the flames will hatch the godly soul will over time scratch. Time, you will find overlaps and it seems to turn back you relapse. Asking for forgiveness but the Devil comes your business. Wealth tightens down like a belt cursing yourself from what you dealt. The money will soon melt then what can you conclude to God? How can you prove what shall you do in life to do things right and not rot? Love living to amuse now outcast a fool. Beaten people cruel broken multiple rules. For say a pair of shoes this poisons humanity, you and I Can't you see? Being wealthy promotes most souls unhealthy.

264.   Nightfall sky: At night the beautiful site look out and recognize the nightfall sky. As dark as can be stars multiply, shining bright as high as a kite there gloomy and far as the sun disappears making the sky clear. Each star I see there are small but visible to see you and me. As the day leaves a new half make believe. As time fly's by oh my, do you see the nightfall sky?

265.   Day after day: Day after day to God I shall pray after day we conversate as moments escalade. Soon the pain will fade although I cannot always hear what you say you still speak to me some way. I lie on you in this journey to give me a hand. Let me understand that there's always a way that we can make change Begin. I hate that I continue to sin the Devil provoking me to be his friend. I just hope to see you in the end in Heaven shall I blend. Times is pending and life is real. There's no pretending what shall come out as a flower will sprout. I shall hold no doubt each day I count. The clock is ticking for my existence. Rather I achieve and believe in the end what shall I receive? What philosophies will I conceive? When I leave who will remember and believe me? It isn't easy being free and in this world too blind to see what's ahead of all of we. Before I go I have one last prayer to pray and special words to say. If I should die before I wake I hope my soul God's confiscates and make a space in Heaven's gate. Where I shall relax and lay but I hope and wait day after day.

266. Love at first site: The naked eye enhanced to a girl or guy perceiving beauty. Body language speaking to be more than polite. It's love at first site. As your heart, they foresight a loving change has bitten on you like a parasite. Sucking away the past and pain what remains. A soul mate too soon to gain. You have to enter a new lane and hope to obtain what's given to you true as the moment concludes. It begins you introduce yourself as a friend. Eyes can tell more than words looks can be superb. Movements can give hints to see if the person shy or seeks to be intimate. Beauty brings motivation with dedication soon there's no separation. How do we know love? Why exactly do we judge about such and such? It's hard to discuss trust but we must look inside the mind. Search to find the past the hurt left behind and recline. How to heel to gain a key to a heart. Reveal the fire burning bright. No need to fright its love at first site.

267. A cold world: Each individual boys and girls all placed in a cold world. On Earth cursed since birth but for what's, it's worth blessings are put first. Each county and city hold something different. From crime rates laws and ways of living. Over a million die over time some killed in homicide crimes. Some in enemy lines at the wrong place and time. There's no promised tomorrow of the clock of existence we burrow. Life's still hollow which follows to every human being you and me. Raised seized to believe peace in our communities but a lot don't make It past their teens. This isn't how it's supposed to be. Soon we will see what leads. I just pray for the people have mercy on each woman, man, boys, and girls we live a cold world.

268. A book of we: Picture this in your mind and set out for answers to unwind. Think of your own life in a book. You are going from page to page day after day chapter after chapter. From when it begins until the end. The cover is a picture of you. The back holds what is a plan for you to do in this book. It's already written by God. As we go through a lot wondering why we are a male or female. Time will tell if the moral of the book will fail. We cannot read this book but live in this book. Of each day, we have taken. Each step prep each line from experiences that define a certain time may be memories of laughter which brings a chapter and soon after. Now that you have a picture but not fully painted let the rest be excavating let my words bring you conversation. So of everything you read you have to have separation to understand this isn't something you can judge by a look. A book was written before the time of us. Listen out and hush trust God is speaking to you through me. Of everything we go through and see. Moments after memories and opportunities. Remember beforehand there's a book of we.

269.   Ocean waves: Looking in the ocean waves puts me in a daze. Somehow there's much to say. I feel like the ocean speaks to me. Although no words I receive. I believe there's a hidden message as God has created and planned. I stare breathing fresh air, so beautiful nothing to compare. For a moment, there's no more pain there. As if the Devil for once spared me. All I see is the ocean right in front of me. It's night but still the sun shines brightly. Time froze for a second no need to fright. At that moment, I ask looking at the water treading fast. It replies and I know why mysterious things still multiply. Finally, I recognize it's us going back and forth stuck in a maze. A part of us in ocean waves.

270.   Statue of liberty: Freedom conspiracy among many. The statue of liberty retribution to the resolution of our constitution. People are understanding each amendment. Some don't condone the unknown for what's hidden is gone. The ways of life rights from wrongs and society tags along. This statue represents liberty pursuit happiness. It's extravagant there's no peace. Which brings madness we can't have this upon us. Do not rush gain trust stand together tough enough is enough. As life is rough from people being cuffed. I'm tired of being treated differently and nothing stands of our statue of liberty.

271.   What you believe in can come true: Throughout the journey of life, there're many things we hope to do. If it's meant for you what you believe in can come true. As the sky is blue and the clouds stick to the sun like glue. Kind of how believing works on you. If there're ways to conclude that the truth will reveal and soon magic will appear. Proving God is near as a human being placed here. To achieve you must believe and hope to see to receive what's rightfully waiting for thee. Like the jack and the bean stock the planted seed. The air and sun with rain will campaign. Soon you will gain and obtain by making the right moves. Yes, there's hope for you because what you believe in can come true.

272.   A happy ending: In the begging we look toward a happy ending. A time where they're no worries no stress and life is at its best. For this quest is truly blessed. Who would guess how life connects to failure and success. It's more than we project because every goal might not be met. The number one things is to earn God's full respect. Let things fall into place when you leave this place there lies grace. An eternal life to face where you are forever winning. Nothing's better than man and women. For a happy ending.

273.   The pursuit of happiness: Through sadness as madness struggling toward the pursuit of happiness. The key to success and survival. Accepting not holding denial of memories in your brain you file. Which starts a trial. To put toward a better state a changed fate a clean slate. Not just pursuit of meeting a mate but to be in tune with yourself. Hoping the dreams come true and not melt. Your fighting for it all but whooped by the Devil constantly by a belt. From choices and experiences dealt you fall down get back up and remain to stand up. Not letting go or giving up. No matter how hard it gets. No matter how many times you think to quit. The happiness part of the road you will soon set. If it gets harder pray more. If you're outdoor try even more. The world fully made to explore but not made to let it all go fall on the floor. It's more than a chore a big wave to escalate in the shore. It's what you are living for. So keep chasing and stay passionate. Soon will come the pursuit of happiness.

274.   People enter your door for reasons: Ever wonder why you met a certain girl or guy? Constantly they come and go by. As more multiply ever recognize how one person can impact you? From words of advice even given to you. To what they do from being around country to country town to town. Different voices and sounds different choices of people all placed in your life. Day after day season after season because people enter your door for reasons. Rather it's to bring change or a lifelong lesson gained. Rather obtain a picture painted but haven't sealed the frame. Race after race name after name things will come out and explain. It may hurt when they leave it may surprise you when they enter your door. For some hold keys to help you experience more. God puts that person in for many reasons we might not know. Sometimes it's hard to let go. The real ones will glow and show. Stay in place and treason. For people enter your door for reasons.

275. Stay away from darkness and avoid trouble: In order in life to be alright walk by faith not by sight. For the Devil shines bright hoping to have you stuck in a puddle. Stay away from darkness and avoid trouble remain safe and subtle. Lay back relax and your life won't crumble. Pick the right crowd where you fit in being in yourself feeling aloud. Listen watch stay alert make little sounds. For God is all around and sins command to the Devil's playground. Now you have the advice to avoid Satan fighting back in a rumble. Stay from darkness and avoid trouble.

276.   Who am I the same as you: What am I worth to you? Someone you hate envy and use? Am I the type of dude to confuse make you laugh with amusement? Am I the right one to choose? Would it matter in your life if I left and you lose? What do I hate to prove? Am I judge by choices of my moves? Do you judge me by my looks style and shoes? What do you see in me and from being around what do you hope to receive? Would you believe me am I the type you like to see? There's a million answers and questions why. I ask God every day who am I the same as you. All a person born for a purpose but we don't know our full self it seems uncertain. You think you know what you want in life don't take all advice because some isn't right. In order to be heard we have to fight! Day by day night by night minute by minute from start to finish second by second you should use your mind as a weapon. Because our brains are a blessing perfection is something we can't taste. A mind is a terrible thing to waste bad habits can put you out of place. Every moment and destiny God is our only recipe. He created us all equally different values talents but all unique. Life's a big competition for every day we compete to show the world our full self. Days are hard barely help but you can achieve stay consistent and believe. From hard work and chasing your dreams you shall receive everything you're after. Just hold memories with laughter. Respect all religions and race treat others how you to be treated. Good luck you shall receive with God believe there is hope for you and me. For there's millions of things to do. Who am I the same as you!

277. A big world to explore: Out there's a lot more a big world to explore. From state to state city to city country to country. All created to hold people like you and me. Some with different laws all stand tall. Different places to go different people to meet more food to eat. Treasurable valuables to keep different shoes for your feet. More hobbies and lobbies for everybody. Colorful trees deeper seas more opportunities. Less and more respect lots of pets and different insects. Let's not forget the world all connects. So go on trips and tour a big world to explore.

278. Aaliyah: A beautiful smile bright as the sun. Your style embraced from race to race place to place and everyone. An angle from the sky too precious for a guy. A voice as sweet as can be. Even though on Earth, you have left we received your legacy. A blessed heart a planted seed with a destiny which reached out to you and me. Your complexion the definition of beauty. A star in life that went far started young and has become one of the best but died young in this quest. You experienced life the best traveled the world. When the plane crashed in a flash that was the last. Seems God called you to Heaven too soon. Many cried oh, God why? The plane hit the waters and started a fire and your time had expired. Gone but not forgotten lost but still found. To those important in your life, your spirit is still found. You died young at 22 with so much left to do. It's hard for someone like you to lose everyone seemed confused and cried many whys. But accepted to God, you have flown to. No more worries no more time a buried treasure to cherish and impossible to find. Gone but to all left empty filled with loving memories. A God's gift to Earth more fortuned than diamonds and pearls. Aaliyah, there's no girl like this girl. Gone to soon a lot in Heaven hope to see ya. Goodbye, Aaliyah.

279. Anything can happen at any place or time: From a person and people going through experiences. We soon find that anything can happen at any place or time. Rather it's a crime a time you find a dime a death upon the streets. A time where you felt so weak seeing the hill is too steep. Steps can be hard to leap. A time where God carried you off your feet. A time where you were cut deep. A nightmare in your dream as you sleep. An enemy that tried to creep. A time to compete there is many places to go things to see. Much time regulated for you and me. But ask God and you will find as life unwinds anything can happen at any place or time.

280. Prisoner of a riot society: If you are black or grew up like me constantly judged mistreated fighting. You are officially a prisoner of a riot society. As a human being, life is more than it seems. We are easy to be outcast put in handcuffs lock up shot dead. Educated but still mislead a voice in us to discuss doesn't bring much. As life is rough going through enough. How can we not give up not see a future not live right? When not being prejudice the others race mainly the white set a green to go while were stuck at red at the light. Treated wrongly so how can we be polite? How can we like and not fight? When we are the type to try to peruse in doing great things. Fall short in depart of communities. A message to you and me a prisoner of a riot society.

281. Drugs sex and money: Life revolves around drugs sex and money. Which can turn ugly it is a disease upon humanity. To every single human being, these things aren't what they seem. People followers and thugs turn into using drugs from hardcore coke, meth, heroin, marijuana, to such and such. Just trust your brain and body will be impacted turning discussing. Sex an effect if you let be met not through a ring when married people get used treated unfairly. A disease spreading upon every human being and money that seems to talk people doing anything committing crimes. It's their choice and fault being taught to have it to survive. Why does so much multiply quickly and fast it goes by. People use you for money act as a friend. You must understand everyone is not a helping hand. God placed these things here for certain reasons. It comes out to sprout holding doubts. Once you figure it out this isn't funny affecting us forever drugs, sex, and money.

282. A lifetime timeline: Past present and future to come. Look how life has now become. We a generation from the 1900's have been especially blessed. But too blind to see how well is for us. Before there was no hope for the poor, slavery, and holocausts. Which has changed and throughout time has come to solutions. But has gained a lot and been through enough still times are hard life is rough. Now we have a change fate a clean slate and fresh start. Hoping with our new president, we won't fall apart. But I see a dark future ahead where things are wrongly misleading instead of becoming better to treasure. Cherish inherit a new road. There's no longer gold no hope barely any fate just awaits. What's going to happen finding us blind? In a lifeline timeline.

283. Obsessions bring depression: Addictions brings itching. Decisions reflecting the way of living. Rather success struggling or stuck in prison. Can you vision an obsession? Rather its success a blessing causing problems to have you stressing bringing depression. Look in the mirror stare at your reflection, your complexion the image of you. What do you conclude? Reflect on what you do and been through. Are you still stuck in a maze a stage and daze to not ever get away? Forgetting isn't letting the addiction keeps you guessing. Obsessions bring depression.

284. The darkness in my mind: As I search in my mind and find the conscious hidden behind. Without light, I still see the site. The darkness in my mind. The sins that lie the Devil trying to freeze me, I'm paralyzed. God has given me pride and provide reasons why. I shouldn't forsake my own life. Although I don't know every wrong from right. It's hard to fight my mind ignites. Then hits light I see the shadow of me reflecting and protecting. But only for so long light will fill the dark. When it goes away it all starts. Then I find the darkness in my mind.

285. Slaves: My ancestors were slaves, picking fields ordered and tortured. It descended later to us still a slave of a white man. For it's a white man world. I'm a modern day slave hard labor working to survive and to my family provide. Jobs are a way the government keeps tracks of our income. They tax us for gas, living, food, and then some. Money is the root of all evil any person will commit a crime. For money slaves before time worked but received no money. In Heaven, there's no money in Hell. Money is paper printed with numbers. The money is colored then passed down to others. "Slaves" my sisters and brothers. A president is a puppet, the government is our master's people with wealth come after. What is a slave? A worker a business man. I'll explain this so you will understand. A slave is a woman or man on Earth not free. There is no freedom free doesn't exist. A mother is a slave to her seeds. Which exceeds to maybe you, maybe me. God was a slave as they killed him on a cross but salvation was brought. This is not slavery! A slave in my eyes is different to me. The truth shall set us free. Until Heaven, we go to and fly away we all are a slave!

286. If we switched shoes for a day: You would see how I pray and conversate day by day trying to find a way. In God's home to stay. As I wait for change hoping to reach fame. Staying in a lane to explore, create a legacy and more to be sure you know I came. Try on my shoes how does destiny feel real? Would you be paranoid or chill? Could you climb over that obstacle walk up that hill? Would you think you won or lose? Now let me switch over to you try on your shoes.

I don't know your background so I couldn't grasp what you been through. If this came true I would then conclude ways to improve your lifestyle. If feeling down on your face, I'd put on a smile. I'll only be there for a while. But own the moment as long as God's condoning. Your soul I'm not owning but loaning. Before all of that, I would look at your own size and strategize. Keep your secrets locked away inside holding pride seeing the difference between you and me? Since I have chosen no need to be confused. For once more than to amuse seeing what destiny can do? If it went that way before we go back relax more and pray. If we switched shoes for a day.

287.   A promise: A promise is more than words and when said fully heard. It's absurd to you how important it is if not understanding lying and breaking one of God's 10 commandments. Just stay true follow through treat people how you want to be treated before you do. It's easy to say but actions speak louder words. When you break for your sake. Be honest because it's easy to break a promise.

288.   Violence leads to sirens: From bad discussions of arguing and fussing to fighting. Then comes violence which leads to sirens. People are too blind to see. Then comes the police putting handcuffs on every human being causing a scene. Now you're stuck in jail. To arrival denial to trial hoping inside survival. It's easy to start a problem but how many talk them down walk away or solve them? Break the issue down and dissolve them don't you understand. That use of words legs or hands can start violence into a plan of sirens? Surrounding your door telling you to put your hand ups putting you in handcuffs drop down to the floor. Reading your rights impolite and more. It's what they serve for to protect. As you're selected to neglect and attempt a bad situation. Applying trouble not trying to be finding but violence leads to sirens.

289.   One wish: As you exist if God gave you a chance for one wish. What would you wish for? Begging the lord praying on your knees to achieve. What's going to change upon you and me a one in a lifetime opportunity? I personally would wish for all of those who have died to be resurrected back to Earth. Who tried and apply girls and guy multiple names. To make a change, there would be a lot of people on this list if it came true I would consist. Dear God please grant me one wish.

290.   Technology: Humanity has completely evolved technology. People have discovered electricity it all grew through evolution. Think of cell phones, computers, television, radios and every technical things. Social media society is sustained to technology. It is more virtual now 3d replicating a diverse a higher depth to assets in life created for you and me technology.

291. Retribution: For those who constantly disrespect God a lot. Not every day obeying or understanding the 10 commandments. Which has started on the evolution of retribution? Although unlike most God forgives and gives any a chance. But expecting a lesson learned it's your turn. Those who are killing, stealing, raping, lying, and dying. Been conniving and devilish deeds multiplying. What's applying is a Devil spirit substitution. Bringing to all who will fall retribution.

292. God's always got your back: Do not lose hope and faith wrongly lack. For God's always got you back. If you can't realize that the Devil will attack, subtract your holy soul. Just so you know never let go never give up stand strong and tough. Soon the pain will be enough. Every day we don't always recognize ways to strategize. Ways to set aside reasons to even conclude why. So I ask why lie? Why wish upon a person to die? Why judge another criticize? Why so fast the time passes by? Why can't we all believe in God? Even though you lay when you wake pray and actually conversate. Take a moment listen what the Lord has to say. It might not come out in words. In time, you will find signs that unwind helping you leave things behind. Read the Bible go to church put God first. For what it's all worth at times receiving the worst. Just accept that God's always got your back.

293. In solitary of my mind: I'm stuck here it seems the Devil would bind. For I'm blind but weary in solitary of my mind. I'll find a way out in time. It is dark here there is no light. Only my pen forms a shadow which leads. It feels like I'm halfway dead with dreads. There wrapped in beads, I'm pulling them out my head. I can't give into the trap or I'll be dead. The only thing that binds me through is my pen and paper. In order to get rid of simplicity, I need a pen and eraser. I hear my lover's voice calling me but it's too dark to chase her. For depths of solitude misleads my footprints. It overwhelms the light for I must put up a tent. How could I intent? A mind is a terrible thing to waste. My own brain I Ident. I abuse misconception for my own amusement misfortune and karma has lent. To be restored I need an angel Heavenly sent. I search for clues holding a horseshoe trying to land it in a straight line. I see the outcome and find. If we aren't divine fate will cosign in solitary of my mind.

294. Bad decisions bring visions in prison: Throughout life Good advice we must listen. Because bad decisions bring visions in prisons. Locked in a jail cell and if you fail to the Devil your soul will sail and prevail to hell, only time will tell. Can you afford bail afford to lose? Based off wrong choices of fools. You see a mind is but a tool like our face but terrible to waste. Erase disgrace and taste a bad fate. Suffering style quitting but wishing. In life, you remain fishing. But outcast the bad or become missing. Bad decisions bring visions in prison.

295.   The alley of darkness: There're no shadows here. For this place is too dark to intimate or regulate. Just filled with dark and hate. Seems things fell short. It's too late a changed fate no gate. But wait how did this even have start? In the alley of darkness. I suppose many are kind hearted but somehow still misplaced departed. You can't hear but see I fear something evil lurking over us. Soon I see this upon humanity a way for us to leave. But in favor of God's greed. Shall this world receive the deed? Which will lead to every human being? That haven't even imaged to have seen. Stuck in between hope and faith. But this is too much hate a road unclear we don't belong here. Hopeless fearless in the alley of darkness.

296.   The right mind: The right mind can always search but find. Read between lines see signs and solve. Mysterious things unwind never looking behind. In time will redefine their state of a mind. The picture they paint each memory has passed. Since the mind is a terrible thing to waste. They adapt to this place holding grace but lace Just look at sites outer space. They erase any pain only looks to gain and remain sane. All in one lane. Auto piolet on their own plane. The one who the Devil can't provoke or find the right mind.

297.   Selling your soul: Selling your soul is letting go, and letting God know you can't no longer follow his plan. Hold his hand and stay on his road. For you are too blind to see and know life is gold. So you dig a hole putting your spirit in a hole with a shovel. Then worship the Devil since Satan is waiting being patient. Once done congratulation giving you dark conversations to prevail burn in hell. Time won't tell to the end on judgment day when to God you have failed. He has trapped you in a cell to burn in hell. For you have thrown away the grace of God. Hidden in the sun let the full moon sprung soon to be hung up on you. Nothing to do or conclude you lose. What the Devil wants you to do. "God let him go he or she is with me" and now you're selling your soul.

298.   Ashes to ashes dust to dust: You have been through enough. Time is up ashes dust to dust. For u must not rush but listen for God's voice and hush. Soon you will leave and heaven if lived life rightfully succeeds. This is a plan for you and me. As death, we one day will see. Let it be for the Lord has showed us mercy. The ashes fall into the dust. As for our family and peers tears bust. But trust we have won not failed. To God, we have prevailed. Only time will tell what's life after death for us. Ashes to ashes dust to dust.

299.   A broken window: A broken window is a broken mirror. A broken heart temporally is torn apart. The reflection has failed impelled to Intel. What lies inside a solitary mind? For broken promises are left behind. But in time, the pieces will come back together. Fall back into place and what is broken will erase. As the sun glares and chase. The darkness within resembles resurrecting a broken window.

300. A path of blessings: Based on obsessions of your selections. Which brings collections. Leading to a path of blessings. Lifelong lessons some can keep you guessing bringing depressions. Our existence is precious at time ticks we human being that still exist. Life equips many paths and roads things we don't expect to know. Things we let go we walk run stumble hoping not to crumble. At times fumble fighting the Devil in a rumble. With God being humble seeing up ahead. But if not walking by faith and not by sight. Mislead to prison in the mind conscious being misread in the head. Instead, what is rightfully earned throughout experiences we learn? It's going be all our turns addressing a path of blessings.

301. A lesson to learn: A lesson to learn is a blessing earned. Once the course plays it's turn. It will then confirm as the fire burns your soul. Letting you know that's a no let that habit go and take control of your actions. Let each choice bring satisfaction and a good reaction, not a distraction. For we are not perfect met to sin but trends will begin it blends for every woman and man to be a concern for a lesson to learn.

302. Amen: Lord I just want to thank you for right now and every second to come. The man I will become I love you. Each day more and more. I pray to you on my hand knees and feet. As I wait for you to speak. I'm not perfect but a growing men met to sin. As the pain begins I thread the needle in my skin. Hoping not to do wrong again. For each lie, I hope you forgive me I apologize. But still haven't realized the spirit of you in me hiding inside. I wonder with curiosity so many whys. As days multiply I've recognized what blessing you gave me. What gifts as I exist all I wish is I see you in the end and not miss. Help me become a right man hold my hand help me understand. Who I truly am lead me to the right path where I'm supposed to be. Please help me reach out to the world with poetry. Show me mercy let my future work out. With you, I have no doubts. Still the world I can't figure out. It's a cold world please Lord help me Find the right girl to marry and have a family tree with planted seeds. Help me achieve as I believe in life I can succeed. As the times exceeds the plan of deeds I hope to receive. Lord talk to me watch over my family. Give us hope and faith make away for another day. Help the world bring to the streets peace. As the Devil try's to seize upon humanity. Hoping to destroy our beliefs. Let us to you reach and teach us more. Help the poor the ones outside doors. Stop this madness let there be happiness, not sadness. Although I am too blind to see everything. Let your eye hide and reveal my 3rd eye. Shall I hold pride and decide to always be by your side. Lord, let me recognize. For when I die, let it be a dying cost sacrifice my soul. To all those who believe in and know. On a cross as it begins. Let me see you with my family and friends in the end amen.

303. Prize possessions: A lifelong obtainable blessing a prize possession. Yourself, a Bible for help maybe fame and wealth. Learning experiences of lessons that were dealt. But, you see most of that is a distraction. Others reactions bring satisfaction. The real prize lies deep inside. As it seems to hide its pride. A guide to help you drive to that particular prize. Soon you will realize what you hold your brain genes and heart. For it all starts to play a part of the recession a prize possession.

304. If only you knew: If only you knew what the Devil could do to you? If only you knew God can only get through. If only you knew each cause has an effect. If only you knew the effect you cause on others? If only you knew how important you are to your mothers. If only you knew how to be true to your lover. If only you knew God is watching but undercover. If only you knew the pain people go through every day. If only you knew there's many with God to converse. If only you knew exactly how to get through them gates. If only if knew that this world isn't safe. If only you knew the world is full of hate. We search to find in time signs and clues. If God wasn't here for you? If only, you knew.

305. Watching over you: I believe that every person in your family tree or friend person that was rightful beside thee. Is in Heaven with millions of things. Every day still watching over you. Not only seeing but around making no sound. But trying to help you put together the puzzle warning you from trouble. Since they ran by rules only can do so much and subtle. Only destiny is designed ahead. You see them in memories flashbacks in bed. Remembering the place and times the words they said it felt so real. As the pain hides away conceal you they could actually feel. Only dreams deceive reality but spirituality is hidden in your mind and soul. Making them impossible to let go. From them, there's an obstacle. They are your shadow the mirrors reflecting you but not making any sudden moves. As them, you have lost because God has chosen to call it's hard to discuss. Still there's hope there still close. At most helping you float. As it's supposed to be but not nearly seeable to eyesight. So to you, it seems to confuse. Just always remember there watching over you.

306. The emptiness within: From all people family to friends. There lies the emptiness within. It all depends on how much you sin. If you say never again threading the needle in your skin. As this disease spreads this sickness begins. It can possess you until the end. A trend which leads nothing to gain no longer the same. Empty is hollow following yesterday and tomorrow of your sorrows. The time of God you borrow is separated planned and regulated. Only deep conversations bring reservations and motivations. To cure this disease upon humanity as your heart turns cold. You're traumatized and froze on your soul you let it go. Not even to know that the Devil seize to control not a crime. More than a sin a law to break but so hard to escape. Even if you wait you still might not make it may be too late. So please do and listen what God says hope to have faith. Pray let the Lord lead the way or your soul will lose control. As it blends the emptiness within.

307. A world full of hate: Cursed since birth living on this place. Every day in a world full of hate disgrace jealousy prejudice towards a race a pace which face of the Devil grace. The opposite of polite sucking the good out of our soul like a parasite. As the sun is bright Satan we fright. To obtain and change sparking the flame eternal life. Of nothing he might provoke to between a spirit of love and peace can be seized. That person will act differently. If God let's momentarily possessed. This quest projects to be blessed but why judge holding a grudge about such and such. Treated bad looked in discuss choose used confused in the end you will lose. If the disease blows the fuse there're no rules no laws for whoever saw. They Disappear, dissolve, and fall then God calls. It's life if it's right in time you will find a line to a gate. Down below the opposite a world full of hate.

308. Into the mind: Look into the eyes read past the disguise. What do you find talk as this person replies? Then lies the truth the real you. Through moments superb for actions speak louder than words. See into the soul even if you don't know true colors will show. A connection like a flower will grow may be fast or slow. Let the moment take control it's hard to scam and read upon thee. Because actually, the man in we the women in she leads unquestioned to no recipe. But enhanced desperately read between the lines listen through the great vines and climb. To a stop at a sign into the mind.

309. Angels and Demons: God and Satan both doing things for reasons. Using angels and demons which prevail when time. Will tell, impel when you succeed or fail. The good with wings sent by God the king watching over everything regulating wedding rings bringing peace. Changing minds giving signs too soon find. Demons provoking to committing crimes lying, conniving, disguising, petrifying, dying, surprising, depriving, and intercepting many blessings. Teaching wrongful lessons doing without questions causing depression. Helping others to be stressing bring forth confessions bad obsessions. To men and women bringing addictions. Angel's words of the wise lie inside. Demons hope to fry telling lies constantly passing by, attacking you and I. Angles share, care not to compare always there. Demons beware pulling hair burning flesh are the best to create a mess creating a test to not let to God be met. Which side will you choose to be under what wing? Satan or our "King" there's no in between. All around

Everyday holiday or season. Everything happens for many reasons because of Angels and Demons.

310. Fear: It's everywhere, close, here, there, comes, and disappears. Fear is near stands clear rather it's real concealed how you feel. Fear of being killed fear of God fear of a lot of fear is brought and caught upon human beings. For this world is cruel and mean a scene and picture wrongly painted. If touched wrong painted excavating with conversation a level of the Devil, enemies, a spider, animals, and vipers thief's deep in a situation and fear of God separation. A future a past our last death to mom or dad the bad you had the mad which makes the Devil glad and sincere to appear here bringing fear.

311. Used: We all get choose and used. Abused, confused, and will lose to prove much to fools being cool. People use people never the less for sex. It connects to complete projects if you let. It will be met lots don't care for respect. It then connects tics tacks and toes. Then the true you will show. How many actually share care treat people fair. So many are unaware who's there to help. Not just for their self to build fame chase wealth consisting with stealth. When dealt although dreams can melt. For karma beats you with a belt. When it concludes you've lost and got choose because a lot are used.

312. Earth: God's doing since birth creating ways for us a nurse and church. To rehearse as Christ reimburse. Human being searched Earth with thirst. Adam and Eve to this planted received first. Starting a generation upon us a family of thee, of we to each planted seeds. In space planets and consultations far. To Earth where we are both the sun the moon circles to consume. Holding our fate if time to erase. This pace Earth a perfect planet planned by God. To hold a lot but small rather adapt to hold life giving back. The sun provides heat the moon gives light and dark. For the both start at different times. But define this Earth of yours and mine. For time will end soon as the meters come. To take out the land before time, not a crime. Which flipped out in a decision of a dime. To find but search this precious place called Earth.

313. It takes struggle: Picture yourself stuck in a puddle. As before you've fumble. It takes struggle fighting rumbles to not crumble. Into a broken puzzle but it doubles as you stumble. It's hard to be humble hard to hide from trouble. Based on decisions of your selections and affections. Which karma is reflecting resurrecting in sections? Reflecting on being depression stressing using mind aggression. Lifelong lessons, weapons, holding, obsessions, and oppression. Left in a challenge accounting. To find a way to a fountain. Not to drought as if it's high as a mountain climbing. On a certain speed but in need to double. It takes struggle fighting rumbles to not crumble.

314.   Manners: Being polite is a gentleman, trying to do things right. Living a way of live. Becoming a woman not just dressing to impress having self-respect. Both use the words please and thank you. Something we should all do. Treat others how you want to be treated. Proceeded more than needed properly greeted, meted. If you do so not defeated, others accept collect not showing neglect. Picture God always watching a world full of cameras. Please use your manners.

315.   Compares: Are you aware that everyone compares. Rather themselves to someone else. From there life to another of what they possess, and anything that comes next. Let's think outside the box for a second. Use competition as a weapon to each mirror's reflection. Others complexion proceeded to be conceited with self- obsession. People can't just be happy what who they are. Everyone wants to be a star in life so far. It's why problems start people fall apart. Broken hearts and parts that dart. Leaving the light just with the dark. As it follows and staying here. Resemble you are still here beauty appears. When you stare but still the world compares.

316.   The hunger: There's no getting younger. For, dreams are scaled high. But picture yourself under. Wanting with the hunger. Life can suck you if not pursuing right like a Popsicle. You strive to climb those obstacles looking as impossible. There is no I can't in a man. Understand for women you can do anything, you can. In the middle is a maze, this trade escalates to you. Provoking moves to solve this equation. The ventilation brings separation. The wind from the fan blows you back. As you act to attack still something lacks, in fact, you react. You wait for the right time. Inside the mind sealed of close blinds. You will then find, ways to uncover the hunger.

317.   Climax: From the prolog staring off into the fog. The stats will dissolve off, all the climax. The end what is brought back, the end? For it will begin for every women and man. Life's too short go by too fast. So many questions to ask. So many memories and laughs. It's just sad we can't cherish every day we have. Shall we be glad not mad. A lot don't make it through each chapter. For us, the Devil is after. The bible holds the truth It's gold by God told. Listen learn use unload staying on tracks. Living a life of facts reaching the climax.

318.   Bullies: Happening maybe right now. Among so many causing frowns. Constantly putting kids down. Making it hard for people to be comfortable around. Others mistreated beaten bleeding crying wonder why. Trying to stop this madness upon kids as they live and give. Why did you not even care or spare? Threating them to beware treated unfairly with cruelty. You need to stop or rot, a message to all bullies.

319. Midnight: No more sunlight, for the clock has struck midnight. The sky is dark the full moon shines bright. Awakening another day of Christ. The terror of the Devil is not polite. How could this excite a life? What can we conclude? To use as advice, we are just mice small. As God stands tall. The sun has left and kept apart. For that's when midnight starts nothing but dark. A time to fright midnight.

320. Why can't we all be friends: To every race face on this place? It is a disgrace that even God's grace can't help each other to spread love everyday. So I pray every woman and men can be sisters and brothers. Love each other be true till the end. Why can't we all be friends? All I see is so many arguing and fighting. Not too much excitement enlighten. Just distortion lost costs like abortions. It takes a heart to love. Following through all of the above. Why not a kiss and hug for we abuse ourselves more than drugs. Even a gangster or a thug can show love. So it's true but why only to your family and crew. A message to you understand pray for my downfall take my hand. Why can't we all be friends?

321. Trouble here: I feel trouble here. I looked at the mirror and stared. Then the Devil appeared. Now I'm aware and beware. As I stare eye to eye traumatized feeling like I'm about to die. I hold my fears and do not cry. I try to put on a disguise and set aside my pride. He decides to try to possess me. I then get on my knees and pray "Lord Take me away let me see another day" I wait then it comes true. What should I do I'm not in Heaven with you. It's cursed everywhere. All I see is trouble here.

322. Stages to faces: Each individual grows from heritage. Ancestors of races and places. These are the stages to faces. Remember when you were young with a smile. It only lasted for a while. You wanted to talk but couldn't utter many sounds. For then you found as you get older. You started forming shoulders. You could warn yourself no longer colder. A toddler and some without a father. How could we see the sites light? When days is much harder. To every woman and man with a son or daughter. Just look at them as they smile. When you holding them but couldn't put them down. All tears that was so much soon disappeared. As they grow older monsters they no longer fear. We are children born and placed here. With a destiny unquestioned separately. Another planted seed to grow up and many blessings to receive. Who could believe, that our childhood memories were the best thing? It went by too fast all right now. Wishing you could start over. Go back after with nothing but laughter. That was years ago with ages. So many changes from stages to faces.

323. Temptation: When I see your eyes, I feel temporarily paralyzed. Butterflies inside but can't figure out what to fully decide. How could you have this temptation on me? Nothing but ecstasy and haven't even went further. Inside I feel loved as a mother. Treated as a brother you're like no other. Watching you converse about such and such. There is no reason for me to judge. You're sweet as fudge. I introduced myself gave you a hug. It's hard to let go but I don't show. Somehow you know I'm losing control. Times goes by too fast. I'm moving to slow. So the way to go is to let the moment play. I get a rose, ''she loves me she loves me or not'' to myself I say I'm Taking the peddles off the rose one by one. We talk four hours you give me your number and we talk every day. You I can't play I watch what I say and pray someway we be together forever. Being clever to take my time leave the past behind unwind away. Hoping to not fail get tails. As I flip a dime in time your motivation. Giving me dedication I'll die if separation. You're heart I cupid dart for location. You got a hold me, cuffed. No need to break the temptation.

324. Please forgive me: Dear god I understand I'm not a perfect man. I never meant to sin as this life begins. I just hope you continued to bless me. For all, I did please forgive me. I feel my spirit empty hollow like a bottle. Help me today and tomorrow past my flaws and sorrows. As holy water, I swallow. Lead me the way God, it's you I shall follow. The road is unclear I feel the Devil near. I try to let go my fears try to hold my tears. I say a lot of things I don't mean. It seems at times the Devil intervenes. Trying to come between break apart our team. Dear father, my king it's time I let the skeletons out my closet. Give away my belongings owning's even my wallet. No more stalling if I don't and won't I'd be a dead man walking. Can you hear me talking? As I speak open the doors I just don't want to feel heat. In the end on judgment day somehow some way I will make my way. Feeling nervous inside don't know what to say. As we conversate you tell me it all. I just hope I rise and don't fall it isn't easy being free. To every little thing every sin I beg for mercy on my knees. To let me in and sorry won't do it. I know my young days being foolish to stupid. I know that I have a purpose of living and reasons of proving for all my doings. I was just too blind to see but lord, please forgive!

325. I'll be missing you: Although you all are gone in Heaven. I'm left in this world all alone. Not knowing what to do. Just know I'll be missing you. Each memory we shared all we went through because it's true. Without you, I wouldn't have the strength to make it never forsaken this placement the dreams I'm chasing. Patient but racing, I know you all are up looking down at the life I'm facing. Watching over me and speaking to me. I wish I could hear it. Still I feel your spirit at times in my mind. I find flashbacks that she left to rewind. As they unwind I'm just missing old times. Though to God, you all filed. This pain makes me cry and realized it is better if I die. So I can see all my family and friends eye to eye and be by their side. Together we will ride my heart goes out right now to my friend who just committed suicide. I guess the pain rained cleared the sunshine. I hope somehow to God you prevailed not rot in hell. Only time will tell and to all my family I hope you feel what I feel. Life is so real I'm so blind to this world. Cursed not knowing what to do. But just, forever know I'll be missing you.

326. When will there ever be peace on our streets: Anger in danger all I see is strangers. "Life ledge when we bled" that's what I said. I got a messed up head. I see a clear path but steady mislead. Reading between lines but find signs getting misread. Why can't the truth come out sprout? Holding no doubts because we all are trapped in a drought. Too poor to put money in our bank accounts. The amount won't count trying to figure out. Why so many dies? So many tears flowing out each other eyes. To life, I'm just blind. Time moves by so fast just losing time. So many committing crimes. How the hell we do not speak out be quiet? When being mistreated judge by the prejudice. Bring peace to our streets! Please, Mr. President because riots, people steady, shooting and fighting. Dear God, can you save us? In God we trust but it's hard to discuss trust. So many will stab you in the back or bust. To every lost soul just kicking up dust. Just pray and hush listen to get away. Life is rough how can we get peace on our streets? When terrorized fools constantly causing beef. Then harassed by the police. All I see is this world isn't for me. That's why it ain't easy being free. Do you feel what I feel see what I see? When will there be peace in our community, to every human being, and most of all peace in our streets.

327. I've loved and I've lost: Of all the pain that will be brought. So many lessons and blessings caught. I've loved and I've lost. Never gave up but fought. Seeing if I can cure a broken heart. As a good man please women understand finding a soul mate is one in a million. So many used the time for a feeling. But I set aside for more. Some man comes to restore. May I gain the key to your heart that closed door? Forever I swim in the sea the open shores. Hoping God will save me no pain anymore. Tired of hearing men call women whores. When nobody is perfect for certain. Another man's loss is another man's treasure. Love is pain, pain is pleasure. So keep ya heads up others will treat you better. If you living in misery of a storm it won't rain forever. Being who I am is not easy. When I try to treat women better. But some are used to they reputation. To a good man brings separation. What is love to you? Some to confused and refuse to let it come into you. Though God created the right one for you. Nothing to do but prove you are handsome or beautiful. Every day blessed individuals. Don't be let down empty spiritually. Men, you can be anything. So to every women and man in relationships with love brought doing wrong. All alone created or caught the lessons will be seen then taught. Just like me I've loved and I've lost.

328. The pit of fire: Admitted to hell because being a liar. A sinner no commandments applying, denning, wrongfully, multiplying, and as your time expires. You exempt the pit of fire beyond stuck in a dryer. Burning but earning what you choose to pick. You tried to change your ways ignored so it's impossible. Now Satan is awaiting there's no conversation. But hell probation no air circulation. The rotation is forever. The pain is not pleasure. The wrong way opposite of up high. Oh, my not met for you and I. You realize you have to hold your pride. Live life right tried to make a way. Pray day by day let God lead you the way. Cursed since birth stuck in a maze of you and can't find some way. You will experience a blaze. In a daze of the Devil's empire the pit of fire.

329.   Death after death: Crime after crime suicide to homicide. When will it rest? Death after death envy our kind as pest. Only God can judge me it's tatted on my chest. I guess I haven't left because the spirit of God is my bullet proof vest. I do accept that one day I'm going to die. Thankful now to survive. When the time comes when I reach the other side. Let me baptize every life. Reincarnated like another sunrise. Me and God together we will rise. Oh, why do so many have to die? So many closed caskets so many tears flowing out of our eyes. Traumatized but deep inside our soul paralyzed. So God even though it's your plan with precision. The clock of existence regulating every women and man. We should thank you every day for living. Please bless me with poetry. To touch the boys and girls. As the earth spins and twirls. When the time comes call or write out a referral. To Heaven or Hell. Only time will tell for who's all left. In time comes death after death.

330.   Don't complain: I know how it feels going insane. Feelings remain but don't complain. Over time with change. Things won't be the same. Never take the Lord in vain. He's the only way to get through your pain. Nobody's perfect or might be the way you like it. Life is how you make it. Through the times you have and the life, you're facing. It isn't going to always be dark. For the light will provide ways to not fall apart. Every human being has a heart. When misery starts it can be tame. Just expect the worst hope for the better, but don't complain.

331.   Lonely: With no one around I constantly found. I hear no sounds my feelings are down. As I feel I'm about to drown which is profound. Nothing but darkness fills around. I still know God is in me but somehow I feel so lonely. Back to the old me with close doors. Furthermore to no key. Absolutely the wrong picture to see. Please Lord sent the right one to me. Friends can't always hold your end. Family can't always comfort. Only this curse can be broken by another the right lover. Like no other each step I take God recovers the footprints I see. I ask the lord why am I still lonely? I see no other footprints besides me. No trace on this place because each individual over time shows hate. I ask God is it too late to walk through Heaven's gates? Why isn't this world safe? He speaks as I wait. I think I begin to hallucinate. Seeing a better state a different fate. He then says "keep your eyes closed but open your soul" I somehow see Heaven a gate with angels surrounding all around. Now this just feels like a dream. How could this be true? "My son I'm with you" and so, in the end, it will be true. I wake back up zoning look around and found. I'm no longer lonely.

332. We pray: We pray when to God its true time to converse. We pray every day. When the road is unclear and we can't find a way. So many ways to pray so much to say. After you thank God u must wait and listen for God's voice. Rejoice then pay attention something may be missing. Or we are not close enough to God. As through life, we go through a lot. God is all you got when I pray I pray for change to have come. I pray for many things that aren't the same. Hoping many blessings and lessons will rain. A signs exchange as this world is dark. When I pray the light glimpse to start. God is touching my heart. Filling up my spirit keeping me from falling apart. I shall hold no regards but let God take me far. As I shine like a star. I shall feel no fear here. For in the conscious of my mind, the Devil will soon disappear. Finally, things will come clear. Each soul reaching out every day on their knees. Praying to God with much to say, we pray.

333. Mind body and soul: Something God has a full control. The mind body and soul. Truth be told without the light of God its cold. Do not worry if to God your soul is sold. Then life is gold mind-brain to gain blessings caught. To everybody with a body the flesh of we now can u picture and see. The soul the spirit of God inside our bodies. Nothing but holy filled right but morally intercepts wrongly. All these factors consist of chapters to after the end. When the last breaths you hear. Everything will soon disappear. Have no fear with God it will be clear. So don't let go. Have control over your mind body and soul.

334. Live by the gun the die by the gun: If I switch shoes with the gang bangers, thugs, civilians and military man. Understand if holding it in your hand you live by the gun die by the gun. From the man, you will become. Shootings to save yourself at anyone. As there bullets shoot out and run. Stopping hearts and lungs killing anyone. This piece you hold in your hand or concealed in time becomes real. Based on a situation of how you feel. Deep inside lies how you kill. You aim showing no shame. Some gain a bad reputation if used wrong to your name. Murder one, attempted murder it's, all the same. Letting others know a problem has started. The Devil has come bullets causing pain a life to drain. A gun you hold and claim. Different in war a purpose of killing is what you are living for. Protecting our country plus many more. It's hardcore a world of hate to explore. War after war when time comes you cannot hide or run. You live by the gun die by the gun.

335. Got to hustle and grind through these hard times: Success is so hard to find. So you go to hustle and grind through these hard times. Picture yourself on the bottom of a ladder trying to climb. As every bill and mistake chasing. It runs the world but not hard to find. Those working day jobs trying to stay in line. In time life flips like a dime. You got to hustle and grind through these hard times.

336. Some can be fake turning into snakes: A lot show hate wishing bad with the Devil and conversate. It seems they taken revenge on a date the cause and effect is the soul mate. What can I say some can be fake turning to snakes? Watching by the interstate waiting by the lakes. To help you have a bad fate. Find a way to close the door of Heaven's gates. Making sure you're not safe opposite of to congratulate. Never forsake because some can be fake turning into snakes.

337. In a jail cell: Just like hell in a jail cell. Barely getting mail and time to wash your tail. You try to succeed but failed. Hoping to make it out but can't afford bail. Dreaming of breaking out but can't prevail. There's no ladder to climb or much free time. A living Hell it's not for us can't you tell? Those in were up have fallen. Doing bad deeds and had to drugs to sell. Just couldn't follow the law. Now u got limited phone calls that isn't all. A penitentiary packed with any race. Barely any space you count down day by day. So hard to pace blind with disgrace. Hit by life in the eyes with mace. Finally, bad reality you had a taste. Looking at letters your family paste. Praying to God hoping the paint will erase. Locked here, it's easy for the Devil to chase. Committed a felony just caught a case. In the court hoping for innocence but guilty. Stuck in a tomb society sweeps you off the streets like a broom. Trapped in a cocoon, this isn't the right place to sail. Only time will tell if you stay free. Or end up in a jail cell.

338. Life can be unusual when you are beautiful: Women are incredible but not viewed essentially. Their complexion is presidential. More than simple it's more than a handful. Life can be unusual when you're beautiful. Other's constantly checking you out your smile and style. They stare glare at what's unfair. What God has blessed you with and shared? So many don't show care not to compare. It's clear you stare in the mirror reality hits. The beauty you have comes realer. To life, you're not a beginner. Maybe a sinner someday you will be a winner. Burn as a star lets lay out the deck of cards of these beautiful women. On a team as it seems thy all are queens. There's no in between why would someone treat you mean? When you look so good and clean. The bad part of a frozen heart is most turn out to be sex Fein's. You are all God's child. So with a smile can change anything. Some day you will follow your plans. What you have sent for indoors of God's residential. Life can be unusual when you're beautiful.

339. Military command: In God's hand as soldiers expand a military command. Protecting our world intercepting. As the police supposedly bringing peace. Never the least fighting for our countries. In every weather, rain, snow, and heat.

America has to compete the number one military system to keep. Fighting wars without sleep. As the enemies creep staying together deep. To us trust there not weak. Always able to seek we watch we peek. Train campaign every day of the week. As the military and president will meet. When the hill is too steep. Obsolete programmed heat. Achieve past any possibilities. Showing responsibility capabilities through abilities. While others show negativity. Serving the world for the sake of you and me. Better than all state because for sure we all are in good hands. Of our nation God which stands the military command.

340. Dear generation: Dear people boys, girls, women, and men. I can't understand the world today. A place with multiple races, faces, stages, all stuck in their own mazes. So many can't solve their problems. Find the answers to their equations. Now I ask why do we have to sin? As life begins my dear friends. The world how do you see? Do you love another, my sisters and brothers? Shall we heal each other? Why do we hate one another? Why is everything in competition? Even with it all, something still missing. Why do we beat up ourselves based on our past? Letting pain still impact and last. Pledge all pray forever on and now that we shall hold a smile. Dear lord, I pray to you for a sign a peace of mind. Please help the world of yours and mines. Help us see the light no longer blind. Let us leave pieces of the Devil behind. Shall I find the reasons to fix madness? Separate happiness from sadness. Lord strike upon me. Why are we judge upon are race and nationalities? So much talent in many and capabilities. So many killed raped kidnaped. The Devil they must escape. Seal our fate open the gate. I pray it's not too late. We must find a way to break this curse. It's Hell on Earth so many cursed since birth. For what I see what everything's worth. There is still hope please don't commit suicide pull the rope. Love yourself in your heart say no nope. Women and girls I see the pain you go through. Mother's all the experiences I've seen. Sex is an addiction but a likely disease. Affecting humanity can't you see? Men, I just don't understand the neglect no respect it all connects to be bets. A try just let's go fetch this shouldn't he how things are set. Thugs using drugs claiming to be crips and bloods. Dying on the streets because of beef. People out that door poor hoping for something to eat. Sleeping on the floor as it rains snows and sleets. Have mercy on the weak I'm not perfect Lord. All I ask for is sunlight to cleanse the pain in the rain which pours. Come into our souls and tour I can't take it anymore. People locked in a cage stuck in rage. Because of a time there life not listening to the right advice. Taking the time to read the first page. Terrorist attacks constantly death. Killing of our world to no one's left. Down to my last breath. When will my prayers be answered? Others dying from diseases like cancer. Lord give me an answer. Please have faith in us life in my eyes is all that I see. All which leads to reality. I shed tears for my tattoo peers. I see the end it is clear. Lord get us the hell away from here. I know you are listening your here. My dear world my dear friends. I hope to see you in the end. I will only call things the way I see. If I'm wrong please forgive me. I'm tired of waiting stuck in frustration. Free us from probation. People addicted to medication. Let all realized the life we are facing. In the end are placement. Help us lord my dear generation.

341. How could this be: Many questions for you and me? Of all I see, everything how could this be? The world of a tree each branch represents we every planted seed. That exceeds from generations past us. Of a life from begging a tree stump. That over time leads to the creator after God Adam and eve. The first two human beings the new life a team. Beforehand things we couldn't handle. Only here for a while, dinosaur's reptiles which got wiped out by meters. A Godly procedure but a misnomer. Denied now God has ramified. The world for you and me. As he speaks and replies changing the world for all girls and guys. Perfunctory through his glory. For he is scrupulous morally. Salutary and renovate today to a better day. Which preclude the Devil ways. Of a stage, that plays to today. We have overcome everything through history. But I still fear no future for you and me. How could this be?

342. Words of the wise: When older guys give advice I then take it in then decide to give it a try. Soon this situation will hit me by surprise like a drive by. Words of the wise that hide in true words as a disguise. When the sun will rise there lies the fire burning inside. My soul as pride I shall slide as I recognition and listen. Thinking to myself what am I missing? Though life is a competition. I see so much different. Each choice shall be made with precision. I have prisons of my mission but wishing. I find the bait the key to the gate being safe no longer fishing. Then comes ambition Politician nutrition. Lifeways ammunition herd don't speak as loud as actions. Only the good things we do can't bring distractions. Opposite of satisfaction, the attraction hits in my brain. Which remains not the same for you and I but set aside lies. Which deprive the words of the wise.

343. I pour some liquor of for my dead homies: I reminisce thinking back to our precious memories. The only thing I know you all are going to stay with me. So I'm never lonely I pour some liquor out for my dead homies. That was real and never phony. Only your grace will get a taste. I'm just stuck in this place feeling out of space. To get out this world, I hope to gravitate. Each step I take each breath I take. Forever our spirits are coherent and won't separate. So I drink to them better days. Hoping the pain will erase. Life's a game but it ain't Sony. I pour some liquor out for my dead homie.

344. The world is created for us to fail: This place is a living hell. Can't you tell? The world is created for us to fail. Succeed to jail but they don't want us to prevail. Have you received bad mail? Or been stuck in prison in a cell. Couldn't afford bail only time will tell. They give us loans on houses to try and own then things go wrong. Which leads to paying all this interest this gives us bad credit. They offer us bills multiply here. They offer us safety but what chance for success? It's fake for Heaven's sake. Why wait when it's already too late? Even though through history, we have been giving new generation's clean slates. We still can't walk past the freeways streets or interstates. The world isn't safe filled with hate. Nothing but ragged competition. Even if you are born with lots of connects of Intel. It's a big possibility not to sell. The world is created for us to fail.

345. A fisher in the sea: Picture we a fisher in the sea. Holding the bible as a key. If we shall die before we wake. Hoping to make it through Heaven's gate. The fishing rod which is God is the bait telling us this place isn't safe. Each wave come across the shore. As this world is plenty to explore. So many keys so many doors to go through. A plan and journey by God created for you. In time, we will get rescue but blind in and sick. While reality hits with the flue. Searching in the water for clues. As we are in the boat it moves slowly. Heading toward our destiny. You and I are a fisher in the sea.

346. Why can't you believe God is real: For those in life that don't look into Christ follow what's right. The perfect advice is this how you really feel. Why don't you believe God is real? The Devil lurks out to kill. Your soul he wants to conceal. Your appeal drills as your mind spills. In your head the conscious filled with hateful thrills. Bad medicine bad pills this assumption is the wrong the deal. For real if God isn't real why do so many believe? Although we are too blind to see. Why do many pray to him in your spirit he won't leave? Although these blessings you've received. As I perceive you're lucky among thee. Can't you see who plans a plan for every single planted seed? Why can't you believe the bible is the truth of life? So many of God are a living proof. When all this turns out you figured out no longer holding doubts. You will be spooked Christ will soon sprout. You will then take unbelieving out. In time as your in line to find what others feel. So why don't you believe God is real?

347. The skeletons in my closet: Of every regret everything I ever reminisced. This is me like all of we the skeletons in my closet I've deposit. Of times, I've sinned and counter plated. Of each and every mistake. Begging for progress hoping it's not too late. Now we shall all stand before the closet door. Holding hands, each soul expand. Back to my life, let's begin. Dear Lord, please open the door. Let me explore he replies "why for? You know you and I can't be side by side my son oh why" I reply just let me look inside. I know the Devil lies there. But I won't die just temporarily a president. Let me into the dark resident. Let me see the Skelton's. I walk to the door stop turn back and God says "what are you waiting for" God I'll be back in four (mins). This is real to the Devil no deal. But I feel nothing can hide. The memories no longer concealed. To get past, I have to forgive to carry on to live as I exist. Please, Lord, grant me one wish. To Heaven, I won't miss. He disappears I walk in it's dark. But I despite no need to fright. Then comes a sudden light. "Satan I have come to see the sins I've done what remains the lessons to gain" Satan replies "this is impossible I can't capture you God's still an obstacle why should I help you guide you through you fool I only want you to lose I've been watching you but can't win even though you've sinned, fine I give in I invite you into my door but my countdown for minutes is four you may explore" I look around then in my mind. As I close my eyes holding my pride. I see what I've done now I can forget and get past that. After flashbacks I pray one more God reacts and sends me back. Now I have shared my secrets with you more than in my wallet. I have buried no more pain to carry the skeletons in my closet.

348. Behind your back: Some people can be fake put on an act. Talking behind your back. In fact, we can't see or hear everything. Something we lack the world is created for us to fail each other to attack. Lives subtract a pack people hold a lot in family and friends. Most don't stay till the end the world blends. Some of those people are the ones who pretend. In your life God sends many people. A lot turn to be enemies but keep your mouth shut open and keep hoping to stay on track. Who knows what's in stored behind your back?

349. The blessings I possess: Not just speaking for me but everybody. Yes indeed in life we hope to receive. The key to success the blessing I possess. Let change, if possible, be met. The goal I set the dreams I hope to intercept. Rightfully you and I in Heaven kept. When Jesus wept tears left died on the cross his last breath. For an eternity a life to begin. Died for all of our sins. Now as life begins I shall blow with the wind. Holding my pride till the end. Forever never defeated but though pleaded. Conceited which will be led. Proceeded still a cursed fate I hope to earn a key to Heaven's gate. Shall God take me in on a date? Praying it's not too late but better late than ever. Right now every memory I treasure love is pain, pain is pleasure. God is in my heart forever guiding me to be clever. Striving for success then connects the blessings I possess.

350. The good times: Stored in my heart. Placed in the back of mind. The good times. Empty of many and any laughs with family and friends. Times didn't last forever blew in the wind. Opposite that, I've sinned when I was born when my life begin. I can't remember the first kiss of my mother. I guess my resurrecting shadow of me is undercover. The good times with my sisters and brothers with many others. I can sometimes close my eyes visualize what's hiding deep inside. I think back the flashbacks as they attack. I'm just stuck in the present but can't get past. I've loved and lost still more pain is brought. When the sun shines I think back to the precious memories of mines. The good times.

351. It takes time to put the past behind: As Flashbacks connects we retrospect in our mind. Even those that are hard to find. Throughout life takes time to put the past behind. Given we are driven in a life line time line. Which cosigns with the past of yours and mines. You're stuck on a ladder trying to reach the top. To not look back but as memories attack you react. Somehow fall back, in fact, those memories can change your frame. Rather good or bad in your heart. Filled with the past the mad and sad. No matter what you revisit what you been through and had. Maybe a family or friend mom or dad. You begin glad knowing life you have. Times move's on goes by too fast. You think the past won't last. But in the mirror as your heart is falling apart. To stop it from starting you must break the glass. Then ask God for a sign to decline. As it will resin it takes time, to put the past behind.

352. Let love change our hearts: Pain stress and agony can tear us apart. Shooting a dart poising our hearts. As it starts let the light come out the dark. Let love change our hearts. May the mate change the pain which remains? Let us gain a fate a key to Heaven's gate. May it not be too late may we find the right soul mate in this cursed place? All the pain will erase no longer in a cage a stage filled with rage. Let light spark outcast the dark. Let love change our heart.

353. White man's world: Dear sister and brothers boys and girls especially for the black. It's hard to survive in this white man's world. They say money is power, power is respect. So how life connects I take what's left. I realize we can't afford to pay for our deaths. In this white man's world they are ones who cut are checks raise our taxes regulating all our steps. What the hell is going on under our flesh and bones, we are the same color but judge by our skin tone? In this white man's world, they put slaves to work. Took away religion try to stop us from going to church. It's hard to say but for a black man we are cursed since birth in this white man's world. They run the government elects our president. I find this evident I'm not saying this in a race's way. We, the people are viewed differently. We're supposed to be equal. In the bible, it says money is the root of all evil. I see the sequel conflicted on our future generation the boys and girls. May God be with you in this white man's world?

354. What goes around comes around: Just know karma is around retaliation will be found. What goes around comes around. It's profound like Harriet Tubman in the underground railroads. Making no sound waves that escalate. That made a way but still you'd drown. In the end, a best man friend is revenge. Which trends as things begin? Cause and effect lends just blowing in the wind. How can this happen again? Treat others how you want to be treated. Then proceeded not to be defeated but pleaded. Jealousy can have you deleted. The gravity holds the boomerang from not counting down. What goes around comes around.

355. Picture my words: As you read my book stress will be taken. Easing your nerves. First thing first picture my words. Every adjective, pronouns, and verbs curve. As I serve words of the wise you probably heard. Poetry treasure buried in the dirt. It cut's deep it hurts as the slaves when they worked. Our minds are tools met for school. But a lot drop out of school. Not knowing the world is cruel. Competition duels close your eyes picture the truth to God I salute. The Devil is a lie hoping we all die. As time passes by asking yourself why was I planned to be a girl or guy? As we try to deny the mirror standing and reflecting you clearer. The end is getting nearer. Life is tangible written in the bible society's manual. Life can be more than we can handle. Too many scandals's a handful. A day awaiting for the Devil to destroy and rule. Here's a clue a message to you. Don't you get confuse with, God you can't lose? There's not much to prove but let him make your moves. Pay your dues then conclude everything. I'm explaining to you life's observe. So picture my words.

356. Lord knows: Who ever knew that from the concrete a flower would grow? For lord knows the Devil want's my soul. But God's salvation I will never let go. It's nothing but Hell here. So many on food stamps and welfare. Why can't we all share all show care? Why can't mercy the Devil spare? How much darkness in our soul does the Devil bare? I've used the lord name in vain I've sworn. Truth or dare, dare I'll spare. Truth the Devil I fear. The end is near I see it, it's all clear. Still I remain insane the pain won't disappear. A man's rage is staged in a cage. I'm reading the book of life each page. It isn't all God's words. For scriptures is missing it doesn't show. The secret to Christ eternal life. Only our lord knows.

357. The light: Christ existing throughout life. Guiding others right something we can't but fright. A Godly site the light the Devil it fights. Shining over the fire and acquire no sins to begin. A road not to be a liar but prescribe for you and I. To decide we will see the sunshine behind closed blinds. Outside a lost mind let memories rewind. Search for the ladder of life to climb. Be with God in your prime sweet opposite of lime no need to commit a crime. Close your eyes let it hit you by surprise. Traumatize what is hurting inside. Paralyze your pride to glide past this cursed world to the other side. Let flowers bloom and let us reach the upper room. To resume then consume everything with God is alright. You then see the light.

358. Poverty: Placed in this world you and me. We still can't see past poverty. Actually, money is the only way to get through to another day. Though we pray begging for hope. When we fight pulling the rope. Society holding on not letting go. Just so you know when it rains it pours. Upon poor it hails we fall can't prevail. Land in jail can't you tell there's more out that door. A lot in stored for people can't afford. Acquire what they live for picture the tough times at war. When everything went bad crisis upon democracy. We had no time to laugh but the past is the past. Although it still last time moves fast. Help justice the system how could we trust it? End up with nothing with many wealth deductions end of discussion. The rich have something some do help. Dreams melt beating you with a belt. Not speaking for myself but the streets, suffering in poverty.

359. Mother of nature: A tree that grows holding leaves. Before we Adam and Eve. From them, we have received what belief is in Mother Nature? Rain, storms, tornados, and hurricanes. All created by nature descended by God. To put back pain now that we all gain. Lifelong blessings exchange through weather selections. A Godly site complexion of our reaction and affection. May the mother of nature brings rain to help the flowers bloom? As water, they consumed it leaves they sprout. Then the sun shines, we resume time zooms. More things are brought in the nature of Earth caught. I believe the mother of Jesus more than one blessing. Which separates her the mother of nature.

360. The light in my heart: An eternal flame which overwhelms the dark. The light in my heart which starts to ignite each time I pray. Let God cast the darkness in my soul away. A shadow of light to start or living in eternal darkness. Without love I'm heartless. The moment angels condemned on me. I begin to long for guidance desperately. I look at this world and see my eyes must be too blind to reality. Let humanity grow together not apart. As cupid's shoots his dark. It will start till death do us apart the Devil shall depart. As God is the light in my heart.

361. My road dogs: My brothers who provide a certain call. They can see you through any weather even the fog. My road dogs all my friends the ones who will be there, in the end. The ones who haven't judged my sins. Been real not pretend together we blend. Memories multiply again and again. Though we are all not perfect. For certain we are all worth it. Met to know each other my sisters and brothers like no others. Hiding providing if deciding and lend. Recover not morally for a lover. Though lost you by God in my life brought. The lessons I learn the blessings brought. Together many battles to be fought. Even when it droughts I shout. With you, I hold no doubt, not for the money in the bank account. Together we will figure out together we will expand. Pray hold hands create plans to eternity to begin. A message to send fixing each other mistakes. To relate a smog a journey together forever my road dogs.

362. I wonder if heaven got a ghetto: A message to the thugs that haven't experienced much love. The street life was a drug hypnotized by the Devil. Picture this on another level. When homies and family are buried with a shovel. Life is hard as metal but still I wonder if Heaven got a ghetto. A place for the lost soul that on Earth lose control. Couldn't fully listen to God didn't know. Hope and faith didn't show. Still throughout life somehow had to grow. The pain as it remains hope to let go. Will there be a way to rise glide set aside? But still consume a spot in an upper room on the other side. Will God let those involved to rot burn in Hell dissolve but somehow call? Though everyone deserves to be forgiven. Rightfully were all God's children. Sinning like in the begging. Though the life we resemble assemble. Can we still live our everyday life? Separate this world but hail to our king through rings bring our wife. Though lived all the way right. Lord, please provide light because the Devil is so hard to fight. We aren't perfect cursed since birth. But search for where to tremble and peddle. I wonder if Heaven got a ghetto.

363. Life is rough: We all go through a lot just hard times. So it's hard to stand tough life is rough. Enough is enough were on Earth while others are in Heaven, up. With God still can't give up. A time and place with disgrace upon multiple ways. I say a lot when I pray. Hoping God takes the pain away. Until I live to see another day. When I die to Heaven will my spirit fly away? Is just you and I stuck in a hurricane and poverty? How could this be on the streets so many deaths and robberies? So much insanity upon humanity. We the last of a dying breed cursed since birth. To every future seed, all I see is greed. Upon the wealthy with a lost soul. Truth be told still unhealthy. While others suffering crying they won't help me. How could the president be our medicine? Even though the white house is his resident. Still an eye for an eye hit by surprise. I wonder when we all will die. To survive glide to the other side. Let God bring sunshine. Look outside what do you find? People doing crimes locked in bars left behind. Seems the world's lost their minds. Do we provide through hard times? I see heads down please pick them up and pray to God because life is rough.

364. Being free: Too blind to even see the state of mind of being free. Because actually, freedom has come short. Though having wealth fare its Hell here with child support. Poison in new ports life is too short end's too fast like our past. So I then ask do you feel free? Look inside your mind search find your pride. Then deprive the reasons why we have wings to fly. To chase our dreams but they seem to pass by. Few obtain millions try. Still I wonder even with these laws with flaws and constitution. We still suffered abused still losing, lost with confusion. Trying but not doing deceive to be pursuing. Still separation which causes inflation upon our nation. The branches of a life term tree you and I still fall. So there's no being free.

365. Imagine the sky as Heaven: In our eyes, the sky can take up our world. The journey I'm going to take you on is unforgettable. Imagine the sky as Heaven life's reciprocal. The sun is God for we are angels rotating around like Earth. Look at the sky deeply and search. The clouds are different levels of Heaven. For there are so many traits. Imagine a line with Heaven's iron gates. People wait to see out there fate. If Heaven they make picture this marvelous site with trees angels flying in all angles. As you walk in Heaven to explore there lies a door. You take on the tour God is waiting at the table with all who are allowed. For you hold a smile. You find its dinner time this palace is God's kingdom. For there is much more, you see all of your peers you're in tears. Heaven is not the end for eternal life will begin. Outer Heaven will soon lend. The palace is all made in gold. There are waterfalls with holy water animals and all for it is sold. It is only night and day there is no weather for you won't be cold. Angels tell you to put on Heaven's clothes, they are white. I've fantasized this dream this dream day and night. Now you will truly see the ''light'' I can't tell you too much for you will see soon. But at the end of your demise. I couldn't lie can you see? Look in the sky look in the earliest morning when the sun first starts to rise. Look at the sky at night when the moon shines brightly. The site to us can be compromising. Imagine the sky as Heaven with infinite surprises!

366. They say: They say you only live once and life's too short. They say they love but show no support. They say there is a God the bible holds the truth. They say I won't believe till I get a sign or clue. They say the Devil is our enemy and after you. They say love can cure the soul. They say oxygen is the air we bare and free of toll. They say give things a chance let the dice roll. They say evil is everywhere? They say Heaven is above but its Hell here. I say only God knows for I don't really care. You say life's unfair. She says" she can live on food stamps, child support, and welfare." He says "I hate my parents have died and aren't here." We say we feel your pain but most don't really care. She prays to God asking for help. He prays to God but only for himself. I ask God why it so much controversy here on Earth every single day? He replies '' my son soon it will be judgment day their fate they can't escape so forget what they say!

367. The touch of me: The touch of me is Godly still in my spirit I feel oddly. Writing in my diary of the times I've seen. Dear God sorry have mercy bless and touch me. Let others see the blessings caught. Still a broken heart is torn apart. I come to fix all those by the Devil caught in the mix. Which consist as things twist. I see the inside of a girl and guy. Some holding pride ready to die. Most don't know seem too shy. Asking why so fast time passes by? Now listen and hear, close your eyes an angel is here. Let me touch your head. Suck out the pain instead. Only God and the Devil. Which way do you choose? To lead just don't worry you can trust in me. I'm a flower soon to bloom. The Devil is a coward and against me, he will get devoured. It won't take a sec it won't take an hour. Let sunshine clear the rain the pain of the shower. I'll die on the cross the church with the tower. Inside my veins nothing but power. I'll fresh your inside out with the sour. Maybe you don't believe too blind to see. You never know what's can grow through the touch of me.

368.   A shadow of light or end up with a shadow of dark: In your mind and spirit please listen to fatal ambition. Opposite of dissing close, your eyes visualize the words of the wise. Then decide in your heart. A shadow of light to start? Or end up with a shadow of dark. Regenerated Godly separated or on judgment day debated. Down below deflated burning of misery and not overrated. A talk with the Devil or a Godly conversation through dedication separating our nation. It's time to cut deep speak to the strong or weak or those currently and sinning. Please have concentration this is forever no debating. May you walk through the valley the shadows of deaths? Fearing none in Heaven kept or to Hell left. Your soul he intercepts spark of flames endless pain met. Now take a second guess in your brain let it connect. Accept the life you are facing as time is racing. What's ahead though you still survive alive what path will you be lead? When you're dead worship Jesus with conversations or Satan. Unbelievers to be deceive stipulating's wrong motivation. No map, in fact, relocating. Just two shoes that either fit to exist or burn off you. The picture is almost painted. What do you now conclude? Win or lose time to choose. Life's a work of art. A shadow of light to start or end up with a shadow of dark.

369.   Social media: Social media is a virtual world. Real fiction we can't always find. A hallucination in the mind. We spend hours on a computer. To keep up with the world men, women, boys, and girls. As the real world lives. Inside and unfurls how could this be? All these sites so many even pornography. A curse upon thee this information is profound. But not to look in Wikipedia. It's social media look at the history and past. From Myspace, Instant gram, Twitter, Tumbler, vine, and Facebook. The internet is basically people lives. They share thoughts to the world. Take pictures technology is so powerful it can track people's locations. This evolution of social media has evolved to a new world. A bigger picture there are scams. People being killed because of the internet. A true fact the world seems not to know how to react. The web can be used for good can be used for bad. I go back to search for facts in the Wikipedia. Still there's no cure for this curse. Thinking of causes and effects of social media.

370.   The mind of a poet: In life through hard times. Just search for ways to find how to be growing. Morally heroic the mind of a poet. With an open mind a courageous heart. With a story to tell hoping to people, they receive the message it prevails. The morals the Intel all poets are different strive with ambition. Though life is a competition this is different. Maybe you write because something happening inside. Something's missing your decisions with your pencil. Open as you write the begging with a title. Let the words of God let out. Showing to others what life's really about. For me, I push toward to show what's behind close blinds. Line after line I define experiences of others and mine. My imagination positions of hard times. I'm only human not perfect but every day to reach out with words.

From what I hope you all heard. Searching I can be right I can be wrong. I only want this piece of art to remember when I'm gone. These metaphors I write the words I paint. For in your minds as a site a sudden light. Please, open your minds look for signs. I then find many thoughts in the mind of a poet.

371.   The eye of all: God is watching every single human being at all times. Through sins crimes hard times like the sun it shines. The moon is dark life with a frozen heart. When it's full the Devil is at his worst filled with thirst. Although we wonder with so many why's how the world is cursed since birth. Even the church can hold shame but what we don't understand is with God there's change. He forgives there's another chance. So remember of every move you ever made with courage or being brave. Those who witness or people around are not all who saw because God is the eye of all.

372.   The art of my mind: Deaths of altitude based on my attitude. I strive to come from the heart. My imagination searches time after time. For the art of my mind helps define. My pen ignites the lines my soul and heart are created separately but poetically divine. I listen closely to the rain as it pours. I take in the sound of Mother Nature's roar hoping she will devour a metaphor. I'm in abundance with God begging for poetry guidance for my views can be odd. I'm searching for a title a begging till the end. For the direction of my pin spins as the wind. The sun rises bringing bright light. For I'll be awake but sleep through the night. I pray my dreams forsake the sky the stars shall be in line. Once I paint the picture of the sky I shall find the art in my mind!

373.   Menace to society: Based on bad decisions reflecting your background. A good eye of the world you lack now. People fear of you around and the police won't treat you politely. You have been a menace to society. Stealing, killing, labeled a villain. You could have started young just being dumb. Wanting because having none or older your hearts getting colder. Being a bad soldier committing crimes. Selling drugs slanging dimes. Of all you did and been through without obeying God you lose. Confuse of the choices you choose being a fool. Trying to hold an image to be cool. Now you are locked in a jail half way from Hell. Some can't afford bail only time did tell. Receiving mail crying out looking for a way out. It needs to rain wash away your pain. It's dry there's no blue sky it's droughts. You pout and shout it's hard to get a second chance a helping hand. Now you understand the Devil is your fan. Just hard headed couldn't listen live quietly. Now you're a menace to society.

374.   Birds that flock like a feather: People that cause trouble and follow one another. Committing bad deeds together overall it may not get better. Birds that flock like a feather do things with each other. Bringing down another. Do not always follow the crowd. In the future, your choices shall promote a smile. This is how people land in jail. Commit devilish sins and omit in Hell. Only time will tell do not listen to your mind but your heart. Do not get overwhelm with pressure. We do not live forever. Always remember birds that flock like a feather descend together.

375.   The fountain of youth: The water which will wash away your sins. Get in your and cleanse your skin. Let this begin an imaginable truth to God shall we salute. The fountain of youth another way to baptize and save you. What do you do when your whole life you haven't been true? Haven't found God haven't found a clue. What do you do when the clouds are dark gray and not blue. Each sin you have committed sticks on you like glue. Let's not forget God forgives and admit to the way you have lived. Now let it give light in your heart to start. Another chance close your eyes let it hit you by surprise. Relax don't think but drink no need to blink or wink. Let to your soul God link and take over you. For you have a chance to be true. Now conclude and use the fountain of youth.

376.   A path of a maze to connect to a secret treasure chest: A puzzle a huddle a puddle. It's all subtle either one can lead to trouble. Let's think outside the box progress to a way and a step. To a key to God's nest a path of a maze to connect to the secret treasure chest. Yes, finally the pain will rest. This life which is so called a mess. You will collect what be met. To now let your own brain obtain what won't ever be the same. Now to pray to God, you must say "I lay my heart down so please Lord lead the way" For you it will be different so there's no telling what the Lord will say. When you feel something in your heart a tangle in your feet. It will be complete for he speaks. Signs to find the chest to reach. First you have to choose a path. Then ask will my past be erased. Finally, it comes out you sprout but show. You're stuck in a maze a certain light glaze. Somehow God has led you the way kept you safe. You reach the light met then something else connects. He appears and says "for my son you can't take a second guess you will be impressed what you strive to be reaching you must find the secret' your reply will be why? The secret a journey a quest? He replies "yes find the treasure chest I will lead you no more now you may find in your mind to explore" You're Feelings as you're in the sea in open shores. No need to be rescued what can you do? Which way should you choose win or lose? You walk 365 then finally find your way. It's a bright day and God soon will congratulate. Seal your fate clean your slate give you the key to the gate. It lies in the treasure the key you will collect is unfair. Now open and let the sunshine find your way past close blinds. Everything freezes even time it rewinds your temporarily blind. Then the blessings hit you reach success of being met. To a path of a maze to connect to a secret treasure chest.

377. A lost upon a cross which eternal life was brought: A lost upon a cross which eternal life was brought. Millenniums ago for what we don't know since before time. God was let go now we are saved to show. The sun glow the enemy rose. Putting Jesus on a cross a fatal pose. Torturing him took each peddle of the rose. Nothing but pain leads when it begins. In the end, he died for all of our sins. For every future girl and boy soon to be women and men. God sacrificed his only son. To send a message that life's is a blessing. But sins overrule being obsessing, teaching Lessing's, causing depression, and stressing. Once we come before God with confessions asking for forgiveness. Though you watch our eyes are the witness of all our deeds and planted seeds of your business. Each drop of blood you shed now lead to us. Building more than trust teaching all of us in God to never give up. This was long ago now you are a holy shadow still each of us follows. Making a way for tomorrow, not judging are flaws and sorrows. From you, we all borrow your spirit is in each one caught and taught. A lost upon a cross which eternal life was brought.

378. There's not enough money in the world: They say money is the root of all evil cursing us the people. It is because of it, we aren't viewed all equal. There's something the world you must know. Money brings stability which provides many capabilities. It can change you and me the poor admire life more. The rich wouldn't care if it rained or poured. Now some people get wealthy due to talents, business wise, God, or plots. But take this into your thoughts. From all the materialistic things bought. You can't take them with you in the end. Truth be told my dear friends. There's not enough money in the world to buy a ticket to Heaven. When we've committed too many sins.

379. Morals: Throughout life morally speaking of this book life in my eyes. I hope for those who do read to realize. Look at the text look deep inside see what's connects. For a lot will hide like pride. I strive to write poetry with goods referrals plural of many morals. In each poem, I write to define a way of life. Take my advice it might not be right but through God in me, the truth will set you free. Then you will see the blessings hiding in me. Which ignites please don't fright but picture my words a beautiful site. Let my work of art from the start hiding in my heart bite to you I write. Growing on you like a parasite. Soon my talent will take you on a flight. Beyond a kite cutting away the pain without a knife. Your predictions and assumptions of me won't obtain my imaginable height. Through each poem is a message hidden behind. Soon you will find the moral a message separated. Once you read and completed with my poetry you will fill present spiritually. It will absolutely find a way to break barriers and let you break free. I just want you to see this is more than words more than my nerves. As lives curve, each rhyme cosigns with words. I'm not perfect but striving to close perfection of my titles and selections. Through your perceptions so many things in your mind body and soul will be intercepting with affecting. Picture this as music notes leading to vocals symphony's and chorales. I hope in each poem you find many morals.

380.   A day without light: A baleful day a fearful site. Just as night a day without light. The dark clouds overrule the sun just left behind. So there's no light to shine. I then find an apocalypse each soul captured by the Devil. My soul twists I hold on ball my fist in the mist. The disease spreads which consist. Leading to this an abyss. God has left Heaven to risk but the full moon blooms. Earth the Devil shall consume so God will miss. Though he is perfect today even to pray. There are no miracles working but I'm chosen. He gives all his powers to me. Only to hope for light shining bright to receive. The Devil can't intervene with my poetry an outcast shadow a ghost to me. He tries to grab control but let go of me. For in my lines light still ignites. Something the Devil frights it's me and him on Earth. Me fighting for us all for what it's worth. I stand on top of the church. For God to reimburse my soul give me power let me devour this coward. Let the sun shine give light let rain obtain erase the Devil's pain. Everyone around is frozen but me. For some reason there kneeling before for me, God has fused with me. I'm contemplating this can't be true? This must be a dream my king has given me everything. Sacrifice the world in my pen to hope the Devil doesn't win. I'm moving and hacking waiting to be locating. This is tangible no faking I write in the clouds a cure to let down and pass it all around. God comes out the shadow reincarnates he rains upon the drought. He speaks once more gives me a key to open a door. I look at the world he says "what are you waiting for" In my world there's plenty more. No more pain no more misery. Don't worry your poetry will be left forever a legacy. I cry and ask the Lord why? I wake up it's just a dream I've seen shining. A beautiful site, it seems God has foresight a day without light

381.   A day without dark: The sun rose it glowed time still moves fast others are moving slowly. For what's in stored no one but I know. I hold it in not to show still inside losing control. It's time on this place cursed to let go. Finally, a day with the last prayer to pray. The final call of God no more pain to save. May we hold our composers staying sane? Get in line for a daily lane. More than a trip but the dark won't stay and consist. The opposite of a day without light. This is something God shall grant my most important wish. Though I'm still sleep feeling obsolete no longer weak. For some reason no worry. Why hasn't the Devil on my soul try to creep? The full moon is not here for all I see is only light. The dark has disappeared. In this final mission still fishing God speaks I listen and recognition. A change is coming something's different. No more misery and racism in this place. The sun is just not a sun but as it begun. God is in the circle of the sun. I see a smile on his face he has shed his grace. Sealed our fate for a way to Heaven's gate. But before I see something I fright and don't like. The eternal God of Christ on a cross a lost upon a cross which eternal life was brought. I cry my tears flow out my eyes.

He lets the moment play before the end comes for you and I. Though everyone is frozen paralyzed. I still see the look in everyone's eyes, traumatized. Thinking there bought to die. Then everyone angels and human beings in Heaven appears to the sky flying down with me. God is standing face to face it's judgment day. They stand around the king with the crown for I have found. He sucks out the water so we can't drown. Takes all the evil in threading the needle in all who has dirt in their skin. This lens to evolution a problem-solving solution. No more drought's no more doubts. He grab's me we all hold hands and fly away. Beforehand again at last, shall we pray. If I shall die before I wake I hope Christ will reinstate. Dear Lord, may I earn a key to your gate. The line forms now to Heaven shall we reborn. He forgives all gives us another chance. We walk in a sudden light just laughter hearts filled with excite. Angels greet being polite. I drop down to my knees for this I can't believe. I know it has to be untrue what shall I do. Lord, I'm finally with you, you led me through. May the sun shine rise and spring? I wake up from this dream back to reality noticing everything. Still I stand and fight God foresight to start. A day without dark.

382. Good things don't last forever: For better for worse trying to remain together all of our memories we should treasure because good things don't last forever. Even measuring with standards being clever. People change like the weather. Never say never for hearts are broken like a lever a token. In a game of life gain, it will be the over. Only so many lucky ones four leaf clovers. Lots of posers some strive to get closer. Painted picture of a past the things that didn't last. In yourself ask as life is too fast. Lot's hold in potential wearing a mask. For their heart is obscured off regard of pleasure. Good things don't last forever.

383. The needle in the haystack: There're millions of needles in a secret haystack. Only one needle is a cure to the disease spreading on this Earth. For we are forever cursed if the chosen one doesn't reimburse. Walk by faith let God lead the way. There's no practice no rehearse. First you get in though the path of a maze to connect to a secret chest. To collect a map, in fact, to react and attack. The needle in the haystack on the map it lies on the back. To trade the effect of this plague. I then prayed to God I disappeared he temporarily took me away. It's between light and dark the middle of the day. Then he speaks he says "my son you are the chosen one you have to collect the key to life in the chest your book, life in my eyes will progress now try the needle to collect but hurry you only have four(mins) a lifelong reward so what are you waiting for" I walk through a hidden door there lies multiple more. Which door do I enter? The map ends here and I feel the Devil is here. He appears "you have the key in your poetry use your pin as a compass the north, south, west, or east never the least shall you not accept defeat but this task I hope you complete" I close my eyes let my pin provide light and lead the way. I open the door then they're needles in a haystack that lay. I dive in grabbing and bleeding threading the needle in my skin. Seeing the pain of each sin. I then spot something I cannot share but bare. God appears there but I hold no fear. Back to Earth, I shall go back. You have collected the key one of many I have plan for you to receive "My son you're on track the mission is done you got the needle in the haystack"

384. The flower that grew from the concrete: Have you heard of the flower that grew from the concrete? The one which boomed because it consumes the pain of the streets, those that fell weak. It bloomed because the giving tree watching over thee. Raindrop in the crack then the sunlight reflected back. They both fuse to react. The flower grew color representing all our sisters and brothers. The peddles formed representing our fathers, mothers, and lovers. The flower represented many others. But this flower is undercover for no one can see. A secret from humanity created from Adam and Eve. A special seed before the land of time which never did leave. To us on Earth, it was received. Now do you believe in the flower that grew from the concrete.

385. A nightmare: I prayed to God as usual before I laid down to go to sleep. If I shall die before I wake shall God open the gate? It was late that day I dosed off and my dream took me away. When it had started all I saw was dark. For some reason, I felt no spirit of God in my heart for we were temporarily torn apart. I was floating in the sky flying down. But there was no angels were around. I went underneath the ground hearing no sounds. Why wasn't there light for now in me I fright? I couldn't decide to rely on my pride to be alright. How could this be a nightmare I can't fight? The fire assembled the flames started making. I'm close to fainting because there lied Satan. His eyes had flames that sparked I begin traumatized frozen in my heart. He laugh and said "Finally, I have you just where I need you" I thought to myself how the Hell could this be true? All I see is flames no clouds no blue but since the Devil is here I now have a clue. Still I feel I won't lose temporarily I was paralyzed. I saw death right before my eyes. It wasn't a surprise this situation I couldn't deprive. I cried God oh, why? I close my eyes and prayed. I said a poem to the Lord. Then suddenly I imagined he took me away. I open my eyes the Devil was no longer there. I woke up in heaven and God replied "you must have had a nightmare"

386. The end of my demise: I know my clock of existence on Earth is short and will hit me by surprise. In the end of my demise to Heaven shall I glide. Let God decide to let my poetry fly. All of those who are close shall not cry or wonder why. For too fast the time passes by. If I have a wife at that point and time in life that will forever be by my side. I pray we both go together a fused fate or if it's too late Heaven can wait. My journey here the ending will be near. Only Hell I fear and when on Earth I disappear can I forever be remembered here. My poetry shall build a legacy. Place me with all like me who believed Christ we can receive. I wait to die pray not to fry. Seeing an angle in the sky shall we compromise the end of my demise.

387. The angel in my dream: Her smile beyond my imagination. Her hair beyond fashion her presence the main attraction. Her image satisfaction my reaction unconceivable. Her heart unbelievable, just a glance temptation to my soul promotes sexual. The hurt from reading her brings to my heart unacceptable. I tried with words adjective nouns and verbs. Each punctuated curve seems observe my words she hasn't heard. I gain her attention she listens. I strive with pride aim for ambition comfort opposite of dissing. If she doesn't accept or let I must fetch intercept. From the hurt and pain show's her I'm not the same. Here to play no games. Wait, don't leave give me one last plead to speak. I examine her heart notice her feet. I begin to dream because I'm nearly sleeping. Feeling drowsy and weak her I can keep it begins deep. Then comes compliments but none a statement. She smiles my heart beats faster we converse with laughter. I get her number after succeeding the first step that I desperately need. Now spiritual greed I pray for guidance of God to receive. I believe I can achieve I can conceive. Not to hurt or deceive. Just from a smile, she has enervated me completely. I can't get past her appearance my hearts beats no more pain exchanges which bring clearance. Coherent but a patient spirit. How can I obtain and through it all will her love I gain? I try staying insane she has started a new lane a dimension's in my brain sparking a flame. We then and agree to hold hands her trust grows in my heart. I feel a sudden rush I blush the past gets flushed. No more do I regret reminisce or wish. I pray God grant's me one wish. Give me another chance for a future of us in advance. Is this how it's supposed to be? I'm hallucinating going crazy I've realized it's just a dream. I see a door a key my presence flash my request leaves. I see blood on the leaves I cry God why me? Send her back to me. It's flashing I'm close to waking. Damn, I knew it wasn't reality how could Christ strike on me? Which foresight the angle in my dream.

388. The angel that fell from the sky: I had another crazy dream but this one felt true. For some reason, I don't know why I closed my eyes walk outside and saw the angel that fell from the sky. Right before my eyes to catch her I tried. I realized she came from heaven's gate. Seems to disseminate. I stood before her and await I touch her head felt her mind state but didn't castigate. I then prayed dear God why in the middle of the night have you sent an angle from the sky? He spoke and replied "I sent her for you" "I said, I why" "She is the girl of your dream your future queen I have away reincarnated her now I will take her wings in Heaven she has no memory but she is like you a teen for her this will be all a dream lie her down on your bed hold the bible with one hand the other on her head I will give you the key to obtaining her heart for tomorrow morning it will all start you have 6 days to fully obtain and gain you hold a gift a key your poetry may she, you marry have a family tree with planted seeds for this is your deed" I replied back "she inspires me with beauty" God then disappeared for morning I feared. It was 11 pm one hour from tomorrow almost near. She opened her eyes I was instantly traumatized in my heart feeling butterflies. She awoke and said "who are you why I'm here" I replied with a few words we begin to stare. I didn't judge or compare but was glad she was there. In a spark of a moment I heard something God whispered in my ear "her name will not be known for she doesn't remember but u will find it but first you must see how she sprouts" I said in my mind to God "no doubt" her I strive to figure. His voice went away then that very day the connection started to grow. As a flower shall bloom shall the flower grow in 6 days? I come to renovate I hope God doesn't take her away. Together we walked we talked shared our sins our faults. We begin as friends but when I reached for her hand she seemed to apprehend. She replied "you must understand because of my past it's hard to trust any man. I said" I understand but how can I gain your trust I hold a gift in my words my touch? It's been nearly a day you are already my crush. She blushed but we don't have to rush. Though we both done sins have skeletons in our closet towards God don't show denial for God is venial" I knew in my mind u had a 6-day trial. This won't be easy but for some reason I knew she was meant for me. Then time froze the day ended the sun rose it glowed I prayed to the lord and asked God "I have 5 more but how can I gain The reward the key to the locked door" he foresighted us together holding hands on a journey it is his plan I thank God then the prayer end. I must ascend for the 5-day begin. She woke up she spoke more still of her heart I had no control but didn't let go. I tried to console my future soul mate when we touched I fell on my soul she had enervated. We learn lots more of each other sparked a flame to gain feelings for another. Now as a brother the day was close to the end we both lay down side by side and fell asleep. I then had a dream of we, her I actuality did see true beauty. I woke up it was day 4 I prayed to God again then he said "it's time in your heart your let in tell her your poetry by day 3 write for her" The prayer end day 4 begin. We walked we talked begin closer her love soon to gain kept me sane to aloof. In my mind shall one day I have you. The day almost ended we watched the sun fall down. I told her "you are soon to be the one I have found" We walk back to my house and laid side by side. Another dream hit as I closed my eyes. This time, I saw her whole life her past I had no more questions to ask. I woke up prayed to God again he told me "for I have given you both a dream your past to see" The prayer end she woke up again but this was different. In her eyes something I could see it was day 3 I told her some of my poetry. I told her to take my hand fast the day end another dream begin. In this dream on the floor were multiple keys and multiple doors. I didn't know what was in stored but when I grabbed a key walked to a door the dream ended right before. Day 2 begin I prayed to the lord again and told God "will I achieve a key to her heart succeed" He replied "you can you must break free from some dreams you've seen she can be on your team" The prayer end she woke up again but with a bright smile. We stared for a clue it was day 2 I told her "I'm falling for you" she replied "I don't know why but me 2 I now trust you I let down my guard to you" We walked outside the sun shined The clouds were blue we walked we talked. This time, we kissed for her heart is the bait shall I forever fish. Hope not to miss I can't leave her so heaven can wait for her I shall risk. Without her in abyss the day almost end we then committed a sin into me she gave in. We fell asleep side by side then another dream took me on a ride. I was where I was at before I have found the right key the right door. I walk in to enter to explore but woke up right before. I prayed to God again he said "I saw you are more than friends I'm sure you can handle you both to each other act amiable" The prayer end God went away for it begin the last and final day. There she laid she woke up open her eyes I then felt again inside butterflies but held my pride. I told her "good morning sunshine" we kissed then we walked and talked enjoy the day. But today I told her "I have a surprise I told her close her eyes" We watched the sunset and waited by the sunrise she looked I look we both cried I told her "I love you she said "I do to and God has something planned for me and you. Let us go to sleep let the dream foresight" we fell asleep that night. I was back where I was before. I walked through the door there she was the girl I've been searching for. I got on one knee and said "sunshine will you marry me" she said "yes" God appeared and condoned our marriage Heaven we arrived there God said "do you take her to be your wife" I said "yes" Then he ask her "do you accept him as your husband for eternal life? "She said "yes" We kissed the dream ended it wasn't a surprise. We woke up stared at each other eyes by the sunrise. We held hands and prayed to God together I ask "dear Lord is this true? He said "yes I created her for you" We looked at our hands a ring appeared the proof was there in the sun God also appeared. He said, "This is the destiny for you two" and for readers to be continued____

389.   Despair why the world's unfair: To God many don't show care. Even when to you all these blessings he shares. The Devil is all I fear my spirit I have been praying he can't bear. I swear my heart gains pain left to tear. Evil spirits are lurking everywhere trying to get in my conscious whispering in my ear. The end is near in my eyes it's clear. What's joy without pain what's happiness without change. Why is life still the same? Why poison running through is are veins? I remain insane and hope to obtain fame. A throne to gain life's a hateful competition a game. With everyday awaits me to pray to God feeling he is there. On judgment day on the secret chair. The Devil beneath hope to reach our souls and impair. Oh, dear I feel despair why the world's unfair.

390.   The footprints of my past that still last: As I retrospect I see what connects. Still I walk towards success and even though I'm blessed may I still strive to progress. A footprint can show in the snow. Even if planted in the dirt the rain can wash away the trail. Just like the pain when we pray. In my mind, I still see the footprints. The trail before the sins I've done the steps I took with more. Although I'm free and haven't committed a crime I try to walk in a straight line. Still my past redefines what's left behind. In time as If now, I search for answers guidance to break free. Escape stay straight a path to walk through Heaven's gate. May I be forgiven given a clean slate? Forgive but haven't forgotten begging for God to forgive me. As I exist as I predict I still feel the Devil contradicts hopes heaven I miss. Each step I take is permitted praying fully daily regulated the past is the past but to God, I still ask what of the footprints in my past that still last.

391.   When the birds sing: A harmony prior to a sweet melody connecting to a symphony. When the birds sing the angels will call. It may not be summer, spring, winter, or fall. Their pitch exerts to all the trees which provide air standing tall. Compared to the voice of a bird which is not small. A spirit lies in the bird as it recalls reincarnating spectating. Still from human beings no separation. When the ear hears the voice of the birds it comes clear. The end will come it's near as God appears our king. As precious as a ring when the birds sing.

392.   There's only one cure to overcome fear: Spooked wanted to be hunted beware without God impair. There's only one cure to overcome fear. A prayer of the bible because being suicidal is a nightmare. Especially when the end is near. I know you would wonder how and why can I let go my fears. Put them aside rain, rain wash away the pain brings change. No longer dry, a way tide even fear can drown pride paralyze our insides. We then cry asking God why? Only with prayer regenerating the spirit what you are fearing will be coherent over time disappearing. The answers will then come clear. Since cursed here, there's only one cure to overcome fear.

393.   Our minds can play tricks on us: Once our minds are made up were quick to trust. But our minds can play tricks on us our eyes are blind can't see fully straight. We fantasize and hallucinate it's all connects to our mind state. Can hit us by surprise fast or late. Our minds then reinstate reality begins fake. That's when the scene takes its watch and wait for true colors to show. Our eyes glow once our minds know. It's hard to trust because sometimes our minds can play tricks on us.

394.   Ambition: Inside my heart lies ambition. A striving desire to complete what God has planned for me. Prior to my desires of a legacy my ambition blows in ways, I don't know. As the wind, my ambition ends each time I sin. For ambition is a way to see God in the end. A place that I apprehend for I'm not here to offend.

As my journey begins the road never ends. My ambition burns a will as the sun for in time what I will become. My ambition is stuck on me like mold. Truth be told my ambition is gold. When I'm cold the fire burns inside my pride won't deny. Shall my ambition glide when it rains I knew I gave my everything? Heaven will recall the sky will fall the birds will sing. Shall I spread my wings fly above pressure and competition? All that lies in my heart besides dark is ambition.

395. Stuck: Stuck with thoughts was it our fault for sinning as eternal life was brought because God son was lost upon a cross? Each sacrifice pays its price still no advice out of danger. Stuck in anger stuck in misery stuck in the present stuck in our history. Stuck in poetry destined to be the best poet God wants me to be. Stuck on me as I vividly study every human being. Stuck in a dream in between reality and the right deeds for me. Stuck in this cold world especially for those in poverty. Stuck on a journey a road to lead where I should I be. Stuck on life in my eyes what I see. Stuck in the mirror the image reflecting my inconceivable mind detecting. Stuck in my heart lost in my mind. Stuck on fate so little time. Stuck in a circle measuring the degrees of each possible way Satan can attack me. Passionately creating a legacy walking a thin line separately. Desperately I pray for those who read to remember me. The things I predict are not lies to humanity but actually the truth of what I see. A way of guidance for you and me. Stuck in a stage of a maze a huddle leading piece by piece to a puzzle. How can I remain humble when all I fear is trouble? I'm stuck cursed in this world not knowing how long I will last? Every day myself I ask why did I select the choices I did in my past? The regrets forever last but enough is enough still to God I'm never giving up. Till heaven I see on Earth, I'm stuck.

396. Water and fire: When God created Earth it begin an empire and his desire have prior to never expire, water and fire. Water h20 with this life helps me and seeds grow. Fire is the Devil burning on a different level. Water cures fire destroys both to mankind used as a toy. Water used for joy fire used for warmth when we are cold. The spark of a flame is not slow once feted loses control. Water is high and low waves of Earth once excavate now as today and the future plays. As I pray will my skin of the holy water cleanse? To God I give in or see fire the Devil's eyes, in the end, both precious things ascend. Water cooler fire hotter the spirit to baptize our souls or burn hotter than a dryer deceived by a liar. We must look in my eyes of water and fire.

397. If I ruled the world: If I were king sent to Earth a lord of the rings. I would see the light and dark than intervene. If the words of God were written in my poetry I'd be the tornado that wipes the darkness away and twirl. Picture my words if I ruled the world. To the old grown kids boys and girls. You see life is a tree filled with misery. So many cuts of nature left to rest in peace. Just nothing but struggle and fighting the Devil. If misfortune had a heart for than life in my eyes would all start? I look into all souls pray God Holy Spirit and water will help them float. May the holy water be Heavenly sent my rules would bend. It would be evident no more so remember no government no more politics and no more presidents. I would see life provide light like Tomas Edison. To this place if there was a cure I'd be the medicine. Just a nation that all got along the society would be the angels and Heaven would condone. Forever never alone I know we make it home. A glorified sanctuary just as God's home. I call in for support help the poor with prayers as a phone let the satellites. Provide life build clones just prehistoric times ages of stone. Your dreams will be clear never nightmares ascend the stairs no need to beware. God's right here no more worries about flaws and laws. For if I ruled the world I would foresight it all.

398.   Life is chess: In this quest, we are placed a test. Because of competition, it's hard to reach success. Life is chess we strive to progress. One move one step can intercept either Heaven or Hell kept. There're many dreams and goals to have met. Multiple mistakes many regrets we must accept. It's all God's plan set in advance as an individual. Each move is critical what we put in gives it's reciprocal. God is the king the board of chess is the ring. We all are pawns lurking for the break of dawn. The clock of existence regulates each fate. Our slate redefines our place to be allowed in Heaven's gate. When God calls checkmate the road can be straight. For what's ahead we must wait. We are too blind to see vividly and how each piece is a key to succeeding. Open your eyes and let chess be the recipe. The Devil is our advisory opposing necessary accept no defeat. For when we reach glory our legacies have been complete. It's you and I placed where we cannot lead but perceive. Believe to achieve not let grief. In my eyes, I despise this mess. Strive for more naive for less a fatal contest life is chess.

399.   The black hole: This will be the end of time maybe after you and I. the end of our demise will hit by surprise. A forceful field sucking all in not letting go. The Devil will come to Earth as the black hole. A day to fright Satan will suck all in even the light. Even the sun which is bright this will happen in the middle of the night after each soul ignites. The black whole is not polite it searches to destroy with excite. Death will indict a traumatizing site. For it has already begun making its way through other galaxies. Only the Lord spirituality can save you and me. For theirs is a way to leave Heaven to see. The one's too blind to see by the time it will reach. Earth a supermassive black hole will have birth. Sucking all in even the church no more pain no more hurt. Just the earth will burst as the black whole will disperse. What we ever know of our home place taking control. God will console for the Devil will be in the black whole.

400. The 3ʳᵈ eye: In us hiding living and providing more than the naked eye. Vivid precision but foresight to guide the 3ʳᵈ eye. Which is in our souls but remains unknown more treasurable than gold. It's how God watches our every move constantly watching. But also in you we are blind to see but will vividly see. In time once Christ is fully in sinning left behind. The invisible sight will unwind. Once to Heaven, you fly. You will see the 3ʳᵈ eye.

401. The brain of a baby (kid): The brain of a baby is unknown. What we don't realize is there already grown. But puberty hasn't simplicity the growth but a stone. For a barrier puts up a cone. Once born no longer attached to the cordless phone. They see hear and know what's going on. Does not want to be left alone. Their eyes see working high quality. Just as their memory just sprung still left empty. Only temporarily they start off believing in Santa and the tooth fairy. Then more things start to carry they become originated and wary. Only doing what's necessary using their tears and emotions to debate not seeing what's fair. For others grow care start to care it all starts there they now have fears. Beware stair and compare as they grow hair. The clothes they wear the dreams that lead to nightmares. They sleep with their favorite teddy bear. Feeling with safe there a growing heart born in light scared of dark. Analyzing realizing compromising the smartness level is rising. Not surprising God providing have you seen it lately? The brain of a baby (kid).

402. The deck of cards: I regard the probability of life going far. It's probable in the deck of cards. Just as there's only 8 aces a certain amount of kings and queens. We are just placed in between shuffled to now are placement. Which seems are fate shall intervene. This isn't like the old times they're no kings and queens. Just normal people striving for success a business man with the upper hand. A peasant poor left outdoor with many more. Just as God holds this deck of cards, which is life at are stake. A birth comes when the cards shake. Some drown in a lake make it out safe and escape. As people say we are placed in God's hands. Now you truly will understand. I am a jack black but hope to speak facts. The person who keep us from falling apart. Sacrificed his son from the start. God is the king of hearts. One ready to play constantly he degrades hoping we fade the Devil the ace of spades. Up high where the angels stay is the queen of spades. To God, we must pray and heaven hopes to stay. Whon it's all over life plays tricks on us it's simply the joker. I know it's a one in million chance in life to really go far because it's hard. Never disregard the deck of cards.

403. The sky is the limit: Even once you reach the top of the ladder you still haven't finished. In this hateful competition living if you believe you can achieve anything. The sky is the limit but only such time of minutes you only get one life to live. We can't help being replenished but search for the key to success many goals and dreams to be met. Each individual had a chance to be what God sent them to Earth to be. A planted seed soon to grow and see the world's more than make believe. We all have a destiny with our paths separately. It's you and me too blind to see from the begging. Remember the sky is the limit.

404.   Let me free: Even if I'm too blind to see God lurks in me spiritually and to Heaven I hope I see. Let me free spread my wings soar through summer, fall, winter, and spring. Let not even the wind intervene. May this be more than a dream more than a thing on God's team? Desperately I look to see a way for you and me out of poverty. No more being judged by our nationalities. May the flower bloom from underneath the concrete providing peace on our streets? More than the police let our souls God seize. As my actions speak no longer can the Devil creep of an eternal life in Christ no longer weak. Break the chains stuck in my soul deep. Even if I'm stuck upon a cross just let me be. God take me away to see another day. Let me free!

405.   Why should I judge you: Why should I judge you off now and what you been through? We all make mistakes all have regrets based choices you select. We all earn respect in God's home shall we connect. When I look in the mirror my reflection deflects. As my complexion reflects my insecurities intercepts. Rather I accept or won't change in my frame to reset. No matter what perfection won't ever be met. To eyes of judgment being handsome and beautiful is a pet. People have standards they set some withhold to protect. Some who let left vision a treasure chest? Hoping to find the key to beauty not being judged, judgemental free. Why can't we see we explore many things? Love such and such drugs many things we do. Still I ask myself why should I judge you.

406.   There shall be no separation towards education: I don't understand why fools drop out of high school or don't care for college. You need full knowledge learning shall be a dedication. There should be no separation towards education. The future is our motivation the more we learn the more we earn. Once the course plays its turn it becomes our most concern. Without in the end are brains we burn. For schools is a tool the best place where dreams can taste. Without disgrace, a mind is a terrible thing to waste. Society doesn't teach us enough especially when times are rough. Schools don't always help us come up. One life to live no need to rush but we must seize a scholarship or degree learn to be free. Chase our dreams success over everything. Look at the life we are facing deaths left or in prison the wrong placement. Stop waiting start chasing but it doesn't come overnight be patient. There should be no separation towards education.

407.   The day I see fireworks in my eyes: This is more meaningful than the 4th of July. Even though pain hides inside shall to success I glide. Coming up like a sunrise the day I see fireworks in my eyes. Not traumatized just holding my pride and recognize what keeps me from strategizing. I'm going to have to set it aside because it will be a surprise. I do realize it's hard to be humble when going through struggles constantly I stumble but fighting and holding on in this rumble. Hoping not to fumble and crumble. Though mentally I'm subtle praying for the better expecting the worse it all doubles. I see my mind state filled with rage on a page in a stage stuck in a maze. Even with a voice in society still I have on a muzzle. Putting the pieces of the book together to complete this puzzle. Constantly working in a huddle and when the success of my blessings become alive I shall not cry. This is the day I see fireworks in my eyes.

408. If: If I were the sun, I would shine if. I were a clock I would regulate time. If I were a crook I would commit a crime. If I was lucky tails wouldn't fail flipping a dime. If only I could go back in time to my childhood days when I was nine. If only I could forget the past leave it all behind. If I were a flower I would grow if I were the weather I would rain and snow. If I were light I would travel and glow. If I were in agony and pain I would cry. If I shall die Heaven I hope I fly. So many wonders and why's more much than a list. As I exist if God granted me one wish, if.

409. Materialistic things can separate us from our king: Diamonds, pearls, chains, cars, and fancy materialistic things can separate us from our king. We want to be rich so bad but money can't but you happiness. Inside still sad not looking at the meaning of life. What we have you begin lost you begin mad you lose respect for your mom and dad. A dollar bill can't reveal for what God feels. When you spirit leaves you can't take valuable these things. So materialistic things can separate us from are king.

410. Baptize my soul: I accept salvation in my heart baptizes my soul. Forgive me lord let my sins go. Make life new again wonderful like a rainbow. Hold on tight please don't let go on my skin let holy water touch. There is dirt in my skin from the times I've sinned. The texture is rough all I ask for is your trust help me see. For I'm too blind be by my side all the time I give in to you. Please take control Lord baptize my soul. How can we break this curse: Why can't we all put God first? Why does the Devil search to destroy with thirst? When will there be change what remains to reimburse? How can we break this curse? People poor outdoors to survive have to steal a purse. Why are there so many sick but so many cures doctors and nurse? Why do the best of we suffer the worse? The ones up to no good of life are misunderstood. Why everybody is created equal but looked upon different? The worlds hateful with competition. Why even with it all something still missing? Were steady regretting, reminiscing, and wishing. Still to God don't listen. Why does drugs sex and money change today lead the way? How grateful are we when pray? Do we go to church to worship God or we still are hypnotized by the Devil. When can we perceive life in my eyes on a different level? Why are there so many deaths upon are streets? People put for eternal sleep dig in the cemetery with a shovel. No one's perfect but God and he created this world for you and me. Sacrificed his son put us all first still everybody committing sins to God doesn't reimburse. I pray to God every day still without a way. How can we break this curse?

411. Aliens: There among us lurking searching shape-shifting. Those who know are paranoid of these reptoid's. Sucking the life out of people like androids they have their own race, not Canadians their aliens. Studying the human species for centuries but unknown to the blind humanity. Unlike others my eyes bleed I see the different planted seed and believe once earth we leave we will see with our own eyes. As they strategize and capitalize invisible of a naked eye but deep inside lies why. For these creatures are here near within humanity can be any human being. Constantly together divine sending messages to our spaceships and headquarters strange signs. Watching, waiting, anticipating, and gravitating to all require separation. They plan upon our nation the secret behind closed blinds. Soon we will find aliens.

412. Monopoly: Picture us in life but in monopoly. Everyone for themselves chasing fame success or wealth. May be using stealth concealing our health. We all lineup, grab our piece to journey, and seize the mission aboard not knowing what's in store. All of these properties could we afford when those with monopoly are pulling the chords got money and rewards but can't provide for the poor. When it rains it pours take a chance with life learn from advice roll the dice. Maybe to accept Christ or be small as a mice sickened with lice. We explore throughout life follows through but watch every step each choice u choose. Rather a car or shoe win or lose amused to prove still confused. How much will we own boardwalk the throne land in jail or stay low prone dead and gone? Barely surviving or can't afford a home taking the railroads on trips to Rome or blocked by a cone. A row of stone deserted left alone. Which will u own rich or poor finding the reasons to live for one step forward back four an endless encore. May we achieve, may we soar or stuck under the floor? Life perceived by our eye is much more. Can't u see either low-class middle or wealthy? You and I stuck in a game monopoly.

413. The pressure beneath my feet: Of each step I take which separates my fate beneath floating up or gravity pulls my soul down. Deep the fire inside me applies nothing weak but the hill is too steep. I walk in my sleep for God has guidance in me a secret key to breaking the chains of society being free. Respiratory accepts defeat what no human being can cheat of a flame sparking heat. Once under belong deep curiosity lies in me but I'm nervously watching my run the choices

I've done let life rerun take gravity to Heaven of all or burn in the sun. When my life is complete the pressure is underneath my feet.

414.   The possessions of a woman: It's always more than meets the eye. For man don't search for what's hidden stored inside. Some subside, prescribe a way to describe from their hair, eyes, breasts; complexion is scaled to be less met to impress. Only sex can lower stress but women are envied but are blessed. I must confess life is chest each piece confines kings and queens. It would seem one's solitary intervenes which veil in solemn, plural a woman at first a girl. Women possess the blessings to intimate deeds planting our seeds because of thee, it has bloom to humanity. The birth of Jesus the birth of Adam which God then resurrected Eve. The world seems naive which strives to hold and conceive. Not using content to intent love then leave. Women do not need makeup, wigs, materialistic things, and weaves. Their eyes are the guard to one man's insanity thrived vibes which provided vanity. Too many cursed these; women with profanity. It shall not matter, if a mistress is a distress prior conflicted with thickened hips, textured lips, glaring skin, chin: unique complexion soft skin flat stomach not cunning. Men have falsely condemned the possessions of a woman.

415.   Trials and tribulations: Why is justice misplaced upon a race disgrace upon a face? An epidemic spreading upon this place why is there so much hate? A black man committing a crime sentenced maximum time to find a white man commits this same crime let off with probation or parole or completely innocent the situation is left behind. In time, you will and I find how can a black man walk a straight line? It's easier to be a saint in my eyes even when God provides society despise telling us to walk the plank. We barely can afford gas in our tank picture we a fish in the sea but most sink. It's hard to reach success hard to progress when so many are put to death and left. When will there be change when will it rest? A percentage of that make it is like finding gold in a treasure chest. Why because the color of our skin? There's separation we are all equal stated in the constitution of our nation no stipulations just trials and tribulations.

416.   No more: Soon there will be no more pain, no more sunshine, and no more rain. No more of the same, no more taking the lord in vain, and no more flames. No more misery, no more poverty, no need to complain. Rather Heaven or Hell where we will remain? An eternity of light or eternity of fire to gain. No more descendants, no more names, no more births to exchange. No more success, no more fame, no more disgrace upon each race, no more hate, no more fate, and no more of this Earth this place. Either allowed in Heaven's gate walking the path straight given a clean slate. Or to Hell those who God separate flames reinstate. No more deaths, no more take of breaths, no more steps, no more dreams to see have slept. No money, no more rich, poor, wealthy, and debt. The end for you and me soon to accept. From this world who have all left but prayer to pray asking God to obtain the key to that locked door what we have came for. Not accepted placed underneath the floor. There's much to say much to explore. It will be all over soon no more.

417. The touch of music: Music is in the soul music exerts to the heart. Music is light when we are stuck in the dark. Music can keep us from falling apart all the time music is in the mind. A journey through times rather classical jazz r, and b many other before and after that. The sound of lyrics hit's as we react back some to relax. Music is art created spoken from the mind resembling the heart. It comes in deep into you reflecting your mood a story to tell much to use. Lots of words they spoke still in society we evoke. It brings hope words help you float. The sound is the waves the artists are the trade the work of art is the shade. Something we listen to every single day. At times you want to break away and hear something so soothing it's the touch of music.

418. Desperate time's calls for desperate measures: For better for worse for better for better. Each prayer I treasure because there come's times when we think never, but together forever desperate times calls for desperate measure. Each sacrifice pays its price just a way of life. What we prospect what connects cause and effect choices we select. What comes next each step shall be the best especially when life is a contest. We must think first react smart think clever. Desperate times calls for desperate measures.

419. The spirit in we: Something that lies inside every human being the spirit in we. It's sort of like a planted seed soon to grow then God will truly show on your soul take control. We then begin to glow that's God letting you know time moves fast but take things slow. Each time we pray our spirit regenerates we then have a better mind state. A road to be straight a synchronized fate a key to Heaven's gate. May we be forgiven given a clean slate? We must fully give into God be patient have faith. It does not take a day the right gift of God to ourselves to receive the spirit in we.

420. A miracle: It's substantial morally confidential. A miracle with God only can be reached the prince- able a blessing brought not collectible. A thought not because of faults not employed to talk. Actions do speak once seek it begins reached. If misfortune had a heart more than good luck would start the impossible, a miracle.

421. Even in the dark: Cursed from the start even in the dark. God will always be in my heart. I know the light will shine to guide me through right. I will still see the footprints that last leading to my future backtracking to my past. I pray and ask how long this will last? When will I forever with God be divine? When will I find signs access what hidden in my mind? I don't need light to write poetry lines of times before and now, yours and mine. I will still glow the light to my eyes will show then I will know. The Devil can't control my fears I will let go. The dark outcast my ego I'm striving to be let free fly like an eagle. To remain with God forever never broke apart even in the dark.

422. The power of the sun: A fire prior to infinity by God perfectly done. Only God knows the power of the sun. It weighs tons and has become a source of light for life. It has reached unattainable heights. The break of dawn even when it rains the sun does not go. When the moon shines it's not alone the sun regulates time. It regulates the weather there is nothing stronger nothing better. The heat waves day by day send out a trade. So the light will prevail we won't fade in the sun lies. The Lord as he is in plenty more tornadoes as hurricanes that swept shores. The rain which pours but the sun is a stage of rage perceived to be vague. Night by day we pray with the power of the sun. It makes a way when it's all said and done the end will come. The sun will not run for you will soon know the power of the sun.

423. Four walls build a home: Egypt and Rome architecture together creating a throne. Together not alone picture, at first, the roof was gone. There are things to be attached like cordless phones, they measure the width the height everything comes along four walls build a home.

424. All I fear is anger: To the world I'm just a stranger still I feel endangered. The only thing that can set me free is a hanger. Suicide is not the answer but all I fear is anger. Stuck in a maze a stage of complete rage. How can I get through this page? When will the pain go away? Every day morning and night I pray to be let free to find a way. How can I feel at ease when there's so much pressure beneath my feet? My soul constantly cut deep I beg for forgiveness hope for mercy still the Devil lurks to hurt me. My heart is torn apart filled with nothing but dark only poetry can separate the anger apart. I knew from the start I would sin but live life in God's hand. I extol him fully please understand. It's hard being viewed as a black man, not even the sun waves targeting my skin the dirt within can tan. When the madness begins on this place all I see is danger. Till Heaven my soul is received all I fear is anger.

425. Shoot for the stars: Aim for the moon shoot for the stars. Let life take you far a place not met for a car. Out of the world chasing a dream each boys and girls. Sell to the east fly to the coast float throughout the most. Hold your pride keep hope once you obtain never let go. The spotlight will hit the light will come you will know. As you glow one life to live stay passionate be positive. Cherish all that God does and did remain alive, live. Don't regret reminisce life will take you far in mist aim high doesn't miss. As you exist imagine more than who you are shoot for the stars.

426.   Trust none love few: In my eyes, I look what this world has become. I learn to trust no one love few only believe in some. Stay within your circle don't let it break you apart only God and that special one. A lot of people can be fake keep your enemies close and your friends closer most turn to be snakes. They wait to feel safe but strive with greed things they wrongly receive they take. That's when animosity takes its place. When it's all said and done you take none all pain will erase. A message to me and you love none trust few.

427.   Man shall never put their hands on a woman: A man doesn't have the right to punish a woman using his fits. This is why inside I'm pissed! I contradict because God would never allow how can men be dogs and treat women so foul? In my eyes I look at relationships now. If it's bad then on another one must change not the same. It doesn't take a day but you can get away. Women shall pray for a better man and understand. Man shall never put their hands on a women.

428.   It's hard to get our point across: I remain searching but lost. Even though many blessings by God brought. Many experiences and advice taught in society spoken words are hardly caught. It's hard to get our points across. Look at before Malcolm x, Martin Luther king, Rosa Park, many more. So much pain brought the world left sore. something we never ask for. Doesn't matter who you are skin tone right or wrong people don't get along. It's hard to call this place home. When so many who strive for change are forever gone. Who I am the same as you so why should I judge you of what you been through? I search for ways to restore ways to help I don't speak for myself. Even if this book by many is bought. Who would understand life in my eyes, so it's hard to get our point across?

429.   In your voice: Just from noise I can hear symphony in your voice. Rather pain or to rejoice. Rather happiness, sad, a laugh, or being mad. Its' precious to hear a sound of what people have. I'm just glad to be near hear with my ear nothing but bittersweet. How can I fear? It's clear a sound wave from a choice that exerts in your voice.

430.   A mountain height full of dreams: We dream beyond the sky you and me. As time fly's by there are so many why's as everything is not what it seems. Only success can intervene a mountain height full of dreams. A destiny a plan for you and me maybe a clear road to see. Higher above far where the mountains are to obtain is like spotting one particular star. A dream can come true if you believe you can achieve let God guide you through. Trying but not giving up is not enough. How can we lose? We all have much to prove. A different journey different shoes. Only in time, the mountains peak won't block the sunlight the sun will shine on you a sign to redeem. A mountain height full of dreams.

431.   Halloween: On this day it seems for once the Devil has intervened. God is between and won't let things become an ugly scene. As we get dressed to impress and progress. Letting are costumes speak going trick or treat. Our image is handy lurking for fun and candy. I fear our Halloween, the Devil will possess human beings trying to build a team. As God regulates everything a vision the Devil has dreamed of taking over everything. Take over on a dark day spirits he will destroy as the pain deploys. Treating us, all men, women, girls and boys for that is his only joy. May it not work and we all won't get hurt for this day is cursed and mean. Halloween the day of the dead usually Halloween is for trick or treating. But the night before something else occurred in my head as I lay down in bed. Thinking furthermore, my dream took me to shore. I was in a very deep sleep it was dark all around in my spirit I felt weak, obsolete. For some reasons the Earth evil has consumed. This resumed as time zoomed everyone was in costumes but didn't know. For the Devil planned to come up show himself. How did this even come to play? If this was a dream would I be able to God fully pray? Could we conversate when the Devil power is at full state? Well, he takes me away then it happened but not for the better. Everyone with a costume had turned into it this lasted for a day. For chaos on Earth had come this way. But I wasn't prepared, I was writing poetry didn't get dressed wasn't aware. So on me, the Devil couldn't bear. It was like I predicted the end the Devil had possessed every women and man. It begins in midair the Devil had stood. As he was coming down to ground everyone with costumes gathered around. He spoke "Dear world this is our chance to unleash let go destroy the opposite of joy. The meeting started I hid in the mist, for upon this curse I didn't exist. On my soul the Devil missed in this world would he be an abyss. I then prayed to God and ask for him to grant me one wish. I believed so I didn't miss I ask God how can I break this madness? He spoke " you must use magic to overcome this tragic" But how? I've planned this, it's another mission a journey between you and me. For before you have found the way through the path of the maze to connect the special treasure chest. This time, you will be impressed for if found and met to progress. You must go above and beyond now abscond. I disappeared a map appeared I overlooked and stared. I saw the chest there it was for a flying carpet appeared to my eyes prosaic but I looked past it. This is way too much to consume for this situation God has subsumed. Then I arrived at my destination far from others separation. I walk through the door and again my compass became the pin. I enter the door of the east found the key grab the wound God appeared " My son you are one step away now you must say as I say but first in your mind relax picture a candy to give and through the wound attack" I obeyed and step by step God lead the way. "You must take a candy give it to all to break this curse Believe in yourself don't doubt this situation is in you as an individual I created something It will work then put it in an invisible bag for this weapon you shall have" I created a costume that the Devil couldn't consume. Then I put the costume on as he spoke more the Earth he wants to destroy. But had a party before then the Devil noticed he laugh with anticipation. In his eyes spark a conflagration he said "yes I have you now God will today for sure lose it's been you I want to castigate taking away your soul to the gate" But the Devil didn't know over me he had no control he walk away with a smile I waited to react for a while. Then God spoke in my head "switch out the candy use the wound, for now, it comes in handy" I did as God told me but waited for everyone to eat. The Devil returned and told all I have a special treat my special candy they ate it but I fake it. The curse broke and the Devil screamed. The light of God beamed as he appeared to Earth back to hell with you Satan. Together this Earth we restored and told the Devil do not come back anymore! God appeared just as the Devil disappeared back to normal went everything. Then I awoke from this dream for it was Halloween.

432. A freedom song of a slave: Days and days stuck in a cage, a stage of slavery stuck in misery sentenced to be envied. Eternally slaves weren't met to do anything write, sing, or read. For they just put them to work even when there were sick and would bleed. Just to complete their selfish needs for greed which a white man planted a cursed seed committing devilish deeds. Remembering the sounds of the ax hitting the ground. Struggling tired Penetrating digging a whole the heat of the sun sweat running down my skin. Felt as flames in hell family and peers all for sale. Just as being locked in jail days of blackened nights Flashbacks to gloomy sky's. Just guys demoralized a hurtful site. Picking cotton, planting vegetable fields hands bruised bleeding still couldn't yield. All put to work young or old pondering our dreams for they have sold our soul. All for property all for gold endured in the hot and cold. Only this humiliating matter can be told. For freedom is not necessarily free a slave can only dream. Yonder with a voice inside they could not vent but only subside ways for them not to understand. A voice is our pride it shall not hide shall this song help the pain flee. To think slaves had no degree but still learn to sing. To think that slaves had no hope it seems the Devil would intervene. To think slaves were misplaced with hate in times of kings and queens. A man would sing this let me free! Heaven let me in! Foresight my destiny let me see! Pain go away let it rain Lord Cast this torture away. I'm so insane life feels like it isn't real we work, work and work abused hurt no cures no doctors no nurse. But freedom shall hail freedom of this slavery could it bail? Freedom to live freedom to go freedom of pure vanity so much insanity. Lord heal my soul freedom to fly which perch. No disgrace upon race or the church. Closing your eyes seeing I'll forever pay my dues oh! Freedom, freedom knowing this couldn't come true. As a slave sings this in hurt hoping God would abide a clue. Praying and searching for better days in America, the home of the brave the land of the free. Only to feel free you and me? Takes a freedom song of a slave!

433. Until the end of time comes: I live from God presence the light he abides, as he is in the sun. When the dark sparks it seems the Devil would come. The full moon has sprung. Evil is lurking it has begun until the end of time comes. The earth we live on will no longer be fun. I saw this before, again and again for it is our sins which help this madness lend. Have you ever thought, how the world will end? Shall we descend or ascend? My dear friends the world is coming to an end! Heaven shall help for some rules they must bend. The Devil's demon's to the world he shall send. Picture the spiritual world versus the dark side. At a time where we cannot cry. For human can't hide evil, evil cursing the people. The air we breathe may breed rather it's God's deeds or Satan cursed seeds. It will be "we" to fight for our destiny. It will be "he" that shall protect thee (human beings). It will be Satan hoping to retaliate. My eyes are blind searching for signs how can I see straight? Aliens collide Angels are our allies Demons shall deprive. What shall fate decide? A world filled with you and me soon to end as a land before time. How would this all play out? Shall evil sprout? Shall we hold doubts? Shall God scout? How could this all account? This is the future but I'm in the past. I don't know how long we will last. All I can do is pray and ask as life is short, end's too fast. I have no control of future existence none! I just live day by day and hope my destiny is completed, my legacy is done. I will never give up on God for he is in the sun. I shall extol light until the end of time comes.

434. A love and hate thing: What is the principle it's morally substantial? More than feeling the temptation is hard to handle. We got to follow the rules the Lord's manual. Picture this scene a love and hate thing to your inside lighting a candle. In order to hate you must love but things fall apart because of trust. If days by days you are thinking of someone never give up. Time heals all pain the truth will set you free. Because you have a destiny especially the way God planned it for him and her. Life goes on like a movie and if only we could rewind and freeze go back and fix things. Let nothing come between the words "I hate you I wish I never dated you I wish I never met you" In time comes to the truth. It turns on once conceived treated right faithfully then leads to a wedding ring either together forever or separately. Just a way of life a love and hate thing.

435. 3 stages of turning to hate: A love and hate thing all these stages build up soon finality will rain. A campaign to go insane of our fate the 3 stages of turning love to hate. We are created equal each person thinks differently with their brain. Each stage is disappointment breaking the barrier of trust actions then tell enough. For a situation better or worse than exerts stage number two.

Hurt blinding the eyes and pride with dirt. Symphony is weak connection can be obsolete maybe envy. Our mind can play tricks on us what can we believe too blind to see. Once the rage triggers fully the heart is torn apart no screws to hold the brain more than crying then hits pain. Misery, jealousy, agony, more than allergies. How can we hurt one another when we shall heal each other? Once the three stages obtain only God can stop the pain it begins dark. The fire burning inside the alley of darkness within the mind. How can joy we find search for happiness to unwind? Resign to climb the ladder of life to leave it all behind. It's more than poison blood running through our veins the 3 stages of pain. Embedded to a mate, the love turns to evil turns to hate. Even though time heals all pain hate can't escape. Everyone deserves a second chance in advance, for every woman and man God has a plan. God is our helping hand if only you knew and understand once the dirtiness is permitted within. Its stays begins a bad slate there 3 stages of turning love to hate.

436. Never take kindness for weakness: Having a good heart being polite is a way of life. But never take kindness for weakness cutting deep with a knife. Treat others how you want to be treated then led to connections that are right. Thou shall not steal I feel once kindness reveals there's still anger concealed. To each other we shall heal be real. Do you feel what I feel? Actions are the thing that is speaking for many reasons. Never take kindness for weakness!

437. Forever I'm blind: I walk to ascend the stairs walking a thin line. On Earth in the dark light I cannot find forever I'm blind. Searching for answers and signs each step I take leaves a footprint behind. My eyes play tricks just like my mind life in my eyes is an illusion redefined. Just as the secret among society the truth hides. How can that motivation provide pride on Earth? How can I fly be untouched glide provide read between lines spot out lies? As a fisher in the lake how many are fake being rescued to see another day which is not a promising fate. I try to walk by faith, not by site but can't if I do I'll probably faint. It's hard not to be saint we all make mistakes hard to do things always right. The first sign nothing but a cold war visible darkness a poisoned mind. On Earth forever I'm blind.

438. Staring at the world through rear view: Looking at life in my eyes searching for answers I finally found a clue. Staring at the world through my rear view. All I see is the pain we go through. How many victims of the world every day we lose? The cause and effect of choices we all chose. Everyone's searching still confused? All I see is reality as a fuse the sun provides light to life and the moon shines in the dark. I see open minds broken hearts lost souls so many blind. I see the present past and future left so little time. I see the solitary in one's mind. Everything in this rear view mirror is closer there is much more to find. I see a thin line a cold world cursed with me and you. It's me staring at the world through my rear view.

439.   My eyes bleed: Cursed not a planted seed my eyes bleed shedding tears of pain and misery. How could we a dying breed be buried in the cemetery? Searching for lost souls like each word in the dictionary. Hoping my destiny is a legacy which is legendary. So much darkness hidden in my mind forever I'm blind. Searching but what do I find? A picture painted with poetry because life in my eyes is all I see. Believe in me show no envy praying to God on my soul he has mercy. Follow me a message to humanity to those who do read please remember me? So many glimpses of hell family and friends in jail. Some go to Heaven or Hell succeed or fail only time will tell. But do you see what I see? Do you feel what I feel? The Devil is a lie God is real. On every soul he shall heal. Stuck in the dark hoping the light will prevail. I shed tears for my tattoo peers hoping the pain will disappear. I'm having dreams coming to reality asking God why me? I see the end of the world forever my eyes bleed.

440.   It's Dark here but in hell it's hot: Lord brings the light the Devil is giving all he's got. It's dark here but in hell it's hot. No matter where I go I feel cursed in this spot. Praying for humanity to go to Heaven, not hell and rot. So many dying to the streets so many shot. Why has fate untied the loop when God tied it in a knot? To all of you pray for my downfall because at the end of it all God will call the angels will recall summer or spring winter and fall. Even in the dark rightfully with God thou shall stand tall. The cursed will be broke on us all. In Heaven shall we walk? God have mercy on those who fall and rot. It's dark here but in hell it's hot.

441.   Putting someone down: Putting someone down can cause a frown a nervous breakdown. Hateful words are around but I have found. With God in our hearts, we cannot drown make no reactions. Sticks and stones can break your bones but will never hurt you. You must open your heart give into God let his words to your spirit get through. Then you will be rescued. We only can go down six feet deep. Remember words are cheap actions speak. Thou shall not judge us. I'm not perfect and make mistakes can't you see? Living in a cold world cursed then animosity I receive. Why envy me? Equal is what we are created to be but competition brings jealousy. Mischievously my heart can't take any more pain. No more poison running through my veins. Who am I the same as you? So why not treated the same through cause and effect of words you select? What comes around goes around soon to you karma will have found. For constantly putting someone down.

442.   Thou shot not steal and kill: I see life has become real and I feel to humanity thou shall not steal and kill. There's always a cause and effect for choices we select then karma will be met. Mistakes like this we regret if our minds let. This pain we caused upon ourselves we cannot rejoice. Breaking these commandments is a choice. Listen for God ignore the Devil's voice. Look for signs to stay in line think before you act use your mind. Human beings are blind. The only way for good luck to receive in God believe. Follow his deeds use nothing but intensity, to you and me. Don't always act off how you feel thou shall not steal and kill.

443. The end for you and me: I know right now I'm young and too blind to see when you die it will be the end for you and me. Especially when you never bear me I wasn't your planted seed but you took me as yours and so much love received how could this be? I have no memories as a baby I know God has blessed me. To all the pain I've caused everything please forgive me you are the angel that watches over me. Constantly reminding me of my destiny only wanting the best for me. I can't go without your love console on my soul more than above. I see the clock of your existence running thin and this world soon to end. Though not rightfully kin you have let me in my dear mother my dear friend. One day I will truly understand I embrace your grace pray for you every day. Hoping to Heaven God will send you away take away the pain. I'm so glad in my life you have come. Because without you I'll go insane desperately but passionately I cherish every memory. When God calls the birds will sing a harmony a day I won't believe. It's the end for you and me.

444. When the last leaf falls: The time where the end is near the birds will sing the angles will call the sky will fall Heaven will recall. No longer will the trees stand tall when the last leaf falls. Mother Nature has given a sign for her love to end. When it begins the world will no longer spin no more women and man. A time where God will have mercy on thee no more stuck in a cursed place a blessing to see. You and me no more air to share love to care do not beware it will come clear. In our eyes when we have seen when the last leaf falls.

445. Cupid: The ancestors of cupid's bloodline descended down to love. As it seems more addicting than a drug more fulfilling than a hug. For love cupid is the lucky ladybug. His dart is the plug he is blind but the dart always finds the right heart the right soul mate to unwind. Only in time, he is cursed sealed to love as a crime. Cupid is invisible immortal invincible and his dart, aims for a heart leading off the reciprocal upon individuals. It's incredible morally inedible cupid deeds are a handful but he always seems to handle. No pain of a false lover no scandals. Impossible to see as we think one day she will come back to me reality will unfold naturally affecting you and me. He may be young blind but not stupid love comes to life because of cupid.

446. Blood is thicker than water: Air is light as a feather the sun shines bright and gets hotter but blood is thicker water. Thin as ice melting as are days come to end. A way of life family comes second God first. Just as your future wife for better or worse. A seed grows with sunshine and air and just as our mother and father Mother Nature takes care. Our moms bears God has placed you here just as we need water to live. Love our family give over and over again. Friends are campaigns our soul mate can only be so thin but family is there to end. The tree of life grows taller and blood is thicker than water.

447. If you love something let it go: Throughout life if you don't know roll the dice if you love something let it go. Déjà vu will boomerang if so the rest is up to your heart yes or no? Maybe this will happen fast or slow but in this situation, only God can control. People in your life come and go but another soul mate will console. Picture yourself at a stop light green moves on yellow is wait it out red is give up enough is enough but our minds can play tricks on us. If you can't stop thinking about someone every day just enjoy the good times while they last and let the moment play. If one's heart not in it you can't make the relationship reinstate no matter what you say. I know we all have to learn that the hard way. One day even hallucinating thinking one day he or she will come back to us. Though time heals all pain the answers will receive soon to see. The moon will be full if no. An eclipse will start if yes over the sun her eyes will glow. Only time will tell you never know but if you love something let it go.

448. The pain of a false lover: A player secretly undercover like no other treating a women like the gutter acting sweet as a mother. But demand, offend, and apprehend search for intimacy only sex to receive. Man can be dogs understand chasing after cats always up to bat but karma will react. In fact, misfortune will give back. Treat others how you want to be treated but most wrongly led proceeded ego conceited. Thinking just with game any woman I can obtain but not true love is gained. Stuck in a lane always the same. How can one like this wear a wedding ring? How can marriage even be recommended? Only pain gets replenish feelings towards love diminish. You begin to women a menace, a player. Why go for you when their many others? You're stuck alone and lost the pain of a false lover.

449. In time: In time, you will reveal your true colors. Read the book of life even the cover. The experiences, reality will recover we find our path what we want and can't have. The goals the dreams to complete many tasks. We then ask ourselves what will come over me for my destiny. Will I inherit a family tree and treat life passionately, do what God ask of me? I have my journey separately I then find my mind take the bible read line after line find who I am, how I shall strive and climb. We want to go to Heaven but we will see how everything leads in time.

450. Is that u: Is that you, the one who hides behind the clouds which smile is the sun? Is that you, the one who hides her pain in the clouds and the shape is the foundation of your misery? So she has levitated spiritually. I thought of a new way to define you. You emotionally tell yourself you're ok so that's you. The sky is art of your beauty but the sun is imagery of your pain.

451. Love: Love I knew love but not know how? I shall still smile I've been alone for a while. I've asked God to please send an angle down. May she change my frown if I have found. Loves a sea without her rescuing me I will drown. I'm stuck here now karma drowning my sorrows. The ocean is full my heart is hollow it's too much purity for my soul to swallow. Alone today alone Tomorrow. Where may my love be? When will cupid I actually see? Oh! lord, my eyes are playing tricks on me. Has love left for eternity? Or my mistress taken by he; burglary. I couldn't dig out my pain even with surgery. If Heaven be the end how would I omit in? Without my other half my true friend I would be a one wingman. The other wing would have disappeared the road is slippery without my dear. I couldn't travel straight nor steer everything seems foggy not clear. I would contemplate for another but desperation is fear. If only my lovers voice I could hear. Without love death is calling me the end is near. What does it mean to be without love if passion is rationed? I guess promoted without asking love at first site I see no light I live in the night. I lost my love for Years I would fight. My mistakes have been wrongly planted oh! I hate I took my lover for granted come back love I'm so sorry. Dear diary I hate to say this but I feel like giving up years without real love I suffered enough. Only God knows how I fantasize seeing love as a rainbow. I thought through curing one's spirit it would bloom as a rose? I feel lost in a fatal pose I can see still stuck froze. I can smell but love won't detect in my nose. Why can't I just be choose? I been sprayed down too much seems misfortune has a hose. I have seen couples together holding hands but the difference between me and other man a woman soul I'm trying to understand. Deception is a trap sucking you as quicksand. I figured out love connected better for me by holding another's hand spiritually you will expand. As if feelings are levitated fate would land. How would it all plan how? How could I get an upper hand? For love as if now I'm just a fan love is hot I'm in the pot simmering it's so hot. Burning as my heart thinking will she love me or not? I given all I got with another my lover planning a plot. Stars don't shine I must be blind has love recline? I think of memories behind when I felt Heave gave me an angle. A woman with a hidden halo and wings my queen. It seems she doesn't see love with me. One day I over accidentally expressed myself and now the pain she dealt. I'm destined myself to blame? Now things will never be the same. I remember why love is pain the day you left I grew insane. Karma has taken me on a plane a different lane. It's hard to sustain I try to reframe but I feel ashamed. Without love myself I would hang. It couldn't be true life without you a sky no longer blue a sun no longer shining. Love no longer cosigning I could find my love but she'll be denying. I wish I weren't lying I'm dying spying inside crying burning of misery frying. Who is my love, my love is her I Adam she eve an angle that fell from the sky God has sent to me. Mentally, emotionally, spiritually I feel weak. What is love: longing, obliging, veracity, and emotionally. Cupid's dart to your heart love is owning fate is condoning. As we search thus far through stars and consultations it's obliging. As love is kind to human eyes blind. How do we find when life is short so little time? For me and you love is veracity it is true. The only velocity is the Devil affecting you. Physically, spiritually, and emotionally feelings cut deep. It's love resembling we a seed which bloom underneath the concrete. Just a rose love shall bloom may a soul may seek love: longing, obliging, veracity, and emotionally. May it be true from Heaven's above true love?

452. A mind: A mind is powerful but still blank. A mind is created for more to just think a mind is a tool used not fixed. As we exist our minds will always predict and contradict. Have you ever peeked inside one's mind look in the blinds froze time to search and find. How can a mind not retrospect behind? How can a mind collect grasp define? A mind like mine is forever enhanced upon life. Its intercepts advice take out what's wrong learn from the right. A mind is created to fight be polite a mind is created for life.

453. Possessed by our sins: My dear friends in order to apprehend we must thread the needle in our skins. To break the curse as we are possessed by our sins. As the guilt and pain begins the Devil lends a trend of the 10 commandments of life to bend. God Then finds a message to send a sign to receive by you and me. How could this be? It isn't easy being free baptize my soul have mercy on thee. In time redefines the solitary in one's mind forever we begin blind. Crooks committing crimes war begins in enemy lines. Military man expand still in our history is not left behind. We then find the bad habits collects, affects not reset. The cause and effects of choices we select. The skeletons in the closet still left. May our last prayers be prep still in debt on our last breath. To ascend or descend I see the end. We're forever possessed by our sins

454. What does a flower represent: what does a flower represent to you? A resemble of passion Mother Nature beauty fashion? A show of care from another barred without asking a special attraction? A flower to me represents we in my eyes what I see is hidden beneath. I don't necessarily perceive like everybody but like a seed we grow. It needs water to sprout but a flower cannot shout. It communicates with trees through the air and wind they share. The flower blooms once puberty hits some die out and miss. The color is the rose peddle detecting another level. A flower represents peace a flower represents pure beauty but morally reflects you and me.

455. If cupid shot his dart: if cupid shot his dart would it make a way to your heart? Together a start never ever would we fall apart. Would the light shine even in the dark? Instantly, spiritually, and mentally would you be the angel that fell from the sky that God sent to me? Then we begin intimately lovers more than friends. If I poured my heart out to you would you listen to me? Everything seems so essentially, especially when you have a curse on me. Though I'm too blind to see the future of you and me a family tree with planted seeds. Let the sunshine bring rain the flowers would bloom we'd create a family. I'd propose to you, give you a ring yes or no? When it starts make a key to your heart. All of the above if cupid shot his dart!

456. If misfortune had a heart: If misfortune had a heart good luck would start there would be light no dark. If God were real the Devil will reveal a shadow of dark or a shadow of light concealed. The world of ours would still appeal real. I still would see life in my eyes and feel there is no good luck but only destiny. If misfortune had a good heart it would be unquestioning.

457. When the angels call: For the birds will sing the sky will fall heaven will recall when the angles call. Permission from our king may they flap their wings taking our soul away from this cursed scene no one can intervene. Their precious opposite of mean you will be forgiven your slate clean. For it will come clear when your time is up here the end is near. The precious voice of an angle exerts to your ear. For then as she appears taking care of your sorrows now let go your fear. Let the angle fly you to Heaven and steer. More than a dream opposite of a nightmare in Heaven's gate who we fear. God will be there ready to judge sitting on a chair but being properly fair of his grace to any race let in this place he shares. Now u will truly know God cares, God exists you're aware on earth. Say goodbye to them all for we hope you do the opposite of fall when the angels call.

458. The stairs: As I walk by faith, not by sight I close my eyes let you guide me, lord, to be alright. Even though I'm humble sometimes I stumble over my feet. If I should die before I wake I pray my soul God keeps. I feel the pressure beneath my feet still I'm week into deep. The stairs are like hills steep. I'm literally blind lost in my solitary mind progression forward can't go back behind. But in my mind, I search to find the right direction the right key the right door. The right selection for being free is my obsession. Struggling through misery and depression stepping with aggression. I know life is a blessing each step keeps me guessing. I'm searching for a place where he who is there no time to sit and compare. A shortcut lies there out of poverty I'm aware. I feel God here but first I must ascend past the stairs.

459. The ancestors of our bloodline: look at our family tree back in time to the ancestors of our bloodline. Search to find soon to be descendants of yours and mine. The riddle to the puzzle which cosigns to us. This is a must and trust the wind will blow as the dust. There so many branches of this tree straight as a spine. In time, we will all find signs to the ancestors of the bloodline.

460. It's hard to forget when all you do is reminisce: how can I forgive myself even with God's help? It was my choices how situations were dealt. Looking in my heart to all the times I miss. It's hard to forget when all you do is reminisce. Every single memory hiding in me will consist. If I could go back oh, how I wish. To those I hug to those I kiss who could predict pain running through my veins would feel like this. I'm sure like all of you with regrets and mistake there one big list. When will it rest and vanquish my mind just in the abyss? Never know if true foes will turn into a snake and start hiss. I know we all hate to let go hold a composer and an ego. When the mirror is broken then we know. There's a long road with not much to an eye caught by surprise it all doesn't show. I ask God how can I maintain control? A Fisher in the sea please rescue me I can't no longer float destiny in the sea shall I forever fish. It's hard to forget when all you do is reminisce.

461. A sky full of angels: It was the most beautiful thing to have seen I remember it all it was a dream. I closed my eyes after I prayed then dosed off as my dream took me away. It was more than my eyes could handle I glared at the sky caught by surprise as I saw a sky full of angels, flying in all angle. There he was my king the one responsible for this dream God seemed relaxed as the angles sing. He was listening there were no clouds so I knew I found the upper room. But I knew this was a dream not true and would end soon. Then somehow the angles on my heart they consumed. It was like a flower that finally bloomed from underneath the concrete. I actually heard God and the angels speak. I begin weak but felt no more pressure beneath my feet. Somehow I felt complete for they all spoke poetry to me that I am actually writing. I then ascend because I didn't fear of dying. Let me free I felt no lying my soul God conceived I started crying. I prayed as I wiped away my tears God I no longer feared he was there. I open my eyes they seemed to disappear but it was clear. I walk outside only to my eyes they were beautiful I wrote this for you to know. There's a sky full of angels.

462. Plastic surgery: Why is it that people can't accept God's gift natural beauty? Instead, people use plastic surgery to change their image but true beauty than diminishes. This is especially for women we are all equal but viewed not the same once the reflection of the mirror hits the ego change. A lie to your eye of reality deflecting it's unusual being beautiful. A message to you and me God created us with true beauty but wrongly fixing is burglary using plastic surgery.

463. Programmed society: Life in my eyes wouldn't lie to me I believe humanity is a programmed society. High authority makes u see what they want u to see eventually the truth to it all will flee. Lots to this actuality they don't receive. People are naive and many deceive. Many are in their own world it seems people have their own path. So I ask, how much of others reality would you vast? There are billions and billions of people. Think of life as trees every tree has a stomp which spring started from dirt a seed. Then branches form leaves simplicity it leads to how we are descended you and me. Therefore, there are many conspiracies, religions, and race upon liberty. Whatever you believe in can come true. I must ask you what is hidden? What is the actual meaning of living? We are program upon decisions upon nature rules. The mind becomes a terrible thing to waste. What does justice call for in event of crisis which trace? Military command the upper hand seems to erase. The tree of life the ladder to deputies' history has no solution it evolves through evolution. What is here is here for a reason there are seasons things has meaning. People can twist and turn but the meaning behind meaning the hidden cause many will never learn. Knowledge is kept probable costs take its turn. The road to Heaven many preachers and revenue has burned. What is the truth to our beliefs? What is vital to those impeached? So society wouldn't reach. This is something schools wouldn't teach. Only government wealthy high power government seems to breach politics hangman society beneath. The unknown, which is literally ''unknown'' and what is known foretells for the obvious is gone. Whatever is your opinion resonates people take thoughts for mistake. In our constitution there is an amendment ''the freedom of speech'' is promised but to society, it doesn't relate. Many don't believe in fate your life is all you know. Even though my life is just as important as yours that wouldn't be the big picture. What's met for humanity is completing their legacy. So for eternity human beings live in a programmed society.

464. Heal each other: My precious sisters my dear brothers, why do we hate one another? Why envy one another? Why do we kill each other still from each other why can't we be real to each other, provide for another, and pray for another? God was created prior to our desires sacrificed upon a cross lost to reincarnate the world. For Christ begins all God's children family friends and lovers. Let the sunshine clear the rain many blessings to gain still remain not the same. My sisters and brothers, we shall heal each other.

465. Close: Close to suicide feeling so much pain. Close to going insane such a dirty game. None to blame a lost brain. Close too many blessings to gain. Close to God and the world will know I came. Close in between sunshine and rain fame shall I obtain. Let me free to see a Godly lane. My mind is out of this world just aborted a plane. Close to people seeing we are all equal. Predicting the end the world's sequel. Close to hope stuck on faith close to heaven walking through the iron gates. Close to death so little time of my existence left. Cherishing each second coming to my last breath. Close to you hope with poetry God's words will get through you. Close to that key to that locked door. Close to my legacy and many more. Close to being able to fly and soar. Close to my limit dear God I can't take anymore. Physically, mentally, emotionally, and spiritually my soul is cut so deep. Have mercy on us all especially the weak. So much pressure beneath my feet ascending the stairs in my sleep. The last step to ascend Heaven to see, before the Devil try's to capture me. All I fear is anger if endangered respiratory accepts defeat. On a rope nope, God won't let go of my soul a Fisher in the see forever I float. At most humanity will sacrifice their goat. I see the end it's so close.

466. Life goes on: Life goes on: I know soon the world will end but the road never ends. As an individual as my journey begins through my flaws and sins. I am only human I make mistakes. How could I not do wrong? Still life goes on people come and go may be fast or slow. Just as the sun glows heating the world in a certain way soon it will lose control. Truth be told life is gold. I cherish the bible the stories told. Each memory stored in my heart I hold. I shall not regret forget reminisce wish because God has given me a gift. My only wish as I predict Heaven I won't miss. As I still exist I'm crazy in the mind a cold world I find. So little signs so little time. Second after second, minute after minute, hour after hour, month after month, season after season, holiday after holiday, year after year. Still I'm here feeling God's presence near. The road is slippery and unclear it's so hard to steer my dear, the end is here the Devil soon will appear. I'm sincere it's clear but after our generation is dead and gone. Shall the bad be in hell the good in heaven God's home? Will be looking down seeing what's going on. To the future seeds you're not alone life goes on.

467. Self-destruction: So many babies being born reproduction but it's in human nature self-destruction. The world is cursed created for us to fail a living hell stuck in poverty surfing dead or in a jail cell. Only time will tell if to Heaven our souls sell not hell to prevail. Life's secret hiding messages and Intel everything's planned out like receiving mail. The emptiness within has begun. The fire burns inside as we are possessed by our sins. On earth the grim reaper will offend. The black whole will come in the end the fireballs may burn as earth melts. But it's we beforehand who kills ourselves. Guns bringing pain launched to shame upon anyone at any time. Rather retaliation jealousy a crime being in a game and the wrong place and time. It's we soon to fully go insane I see no changes in this world. God has placed every human being for something. Suicide bring's nothing but the Devil still to humanity provides self-destruction.

468. Let's conquer the world: to humanity, hello world men, women, boys, and girls. let's stand strong together pray to God hope for the good accept the bad out with the odds. If I ruled the world I'll command everyone to put nothing before God. Days have run thin the darkness within have begun. Now I ask before this conquest start a shadow of light or end with a shadow of dark. The black whole will soon tear the world apart. Even in the dark together the Devil can't out due Gods fate. Mother Nature whether we must think with our mind act clever. For better for worse for better for better. Each blessing we shall treasure but it only can begin when we thread the needle in our skin. Break the curse upon human beings possessed by their sins. The ten commandments of life we must not bend but ascend. Let God baptize our soul the cure will lend. One voice in society speaks small but a unity the black Panthers will evolve and all will stand tall Thou shall not fall. Time is an existence life is a living lesson. So many why's so many questions? But through depression we must ask for forgiveness admit to our confessions act with aggression. Time will reveal in life if there's a possibility our world will heal. The stipulations will overdue a referral my brothers and sisters let's conquer the world!

469. The Underworld: There's a secret among society many and plural they referral as the Underworld. Label unknown for in the eyes of our own they are gone. Forsake an empire live in a throne it's a certain group not alone. They plan and demand but humanity won't understand the wealth they acquire. The planning of the end as the world will expire. Prior to their merciful desire and acquire their legacy to entire. Their empire they confirm burning fire but untouchable an inflatable tire. The leader the messier has pulled teeth of society with a plyer. Bending rules raising taxes planning attacks on schools the world is cold cruel. In order to win apprehend our sins, we must duel but it's impossible when the needle in the haystack is the fuel. There is a will the power of a mind a tool but wasted misplaced by fools. May this curse be broken upon boys and girls, somehow the chosen one will eliminate the underworld.

470. Outer heaven: I believe once Earth we leave God's still has a plan for thee. They must fully complete their legacy everyone path is separately. First we must ascend this is not just met for preachers and revenues. We all can succeed to see outer Heaven. Beyond out of the world but we must fully be one with God become an angel. There lies a sky full of angels circling around to wait when the times right when God has found. Fate has drawn this process takes centuries but can't take our family and wives. For those are the good times but God will reincarnate a final stage surpassing the to live in to receive. We must believe achieve then an eternal gift God will give. Once our King gives us wings the Devil can no longer intervene. A most beautiful site has seen more than just Heaven more hateful to Satan than to God and all, outer Heaven.

471. Man in the mirror: Sometimes I stare at myself seeing things clearer the end is nearer I see me the man in the mirror. I see a reflection of me searching my soul still incomplete I see misery temporarily happiness. I see pain madness leading to the sadness. I see a future a destiny I think to myself who am I? I close my eyes pray and ask God why then suddenly inside I fly. He replies "my son you are my child hold no remorse let life play its course and smile" I reply I could only smile as a child and I only be on Earth for a while but lord, please send an angle down for my images makes me frown I'm searching but lost so much pain has been brought. He speaks and says "no one's perfect for look in the mirror though it seems uncertain you are worth it only in time you will find shall all pain be left behind in time the mirror will speak to you I will call now repeated my words utter them all mirror, mirror on the wall who's the one that created all there a dimension inside the mirror spiritually tall but not noticed by all now open your eyes but take 3 long breaths what do you see" I reply me. "what's hidden is special you see for perfection is acceptation of defeat life can be obsolete but the mirror reflects humanity desperately searching for acceptance of beauty the wrong thing. I reply my king what do you mean? "Search with your heart look what do you see? A descendant of me the apple that fell from the tree still a seed that's soon to transform bloom underneath a concrete. "Close your eyes and look again is it now clearer" yes! God, it's you hiding in me deflecting we I finally see the moral of my destiny "yes you're getting closer but one more thing take the time to think" I see the end getting nearer I see me with my king the one superior I see the man in the mirror!

472. The ten commandments of life: 1 live for God put nothing before Jesus Christ my advice is only worship one God to be blessed fully right. 2 treat others how you want to be treated treat elderly and orderly with respect. 3 walk by faith not by site be cautious with every calculated step. 4 be responsible for your actions the cause and effect of choices you select. 5 as God said thou shall not cheat, steal, and kill to each other we shall be real and heal to God pray and kneel. 6 thou shall not commit adultery, crimes, bad deeds, selling drugs, and doing drugs to redefine materialistic treasures not met for yours and mine, this is why we are blind. 7 do not interfere with marriages near or anywhere misfortune will appear when God speaks we must listen but actually take the time to hear. Soon you will let go of your fears. 8 to humanity you and I, I bcg you all not to commit suicide! Heaven is destiny for you and I. 9 honor mother and father forever enjoy the memories while they last and treasure. Another love another love is pain, pain is pleasure be together for better for worse for better for better and let marriage last forever. Never take the Lord in vain he is the sunshine which clears the rain washing away the pain. Do not sell your soul for frame. 10 become one with God complete your journey on Earth though cursed since birth for God we must search and see what our lives are worth. In with the good out with hurt when we are buried 6 feet under the dirt. Let our souls fly to Heaven become an angle and outer Heaven reimburse. We must pray day and night search for Christ soon to see the light. As our constitution, we must follow the rules right but most important the ten commandments of life!

473. Judgement day: The end of your demise as to Heaven your soul fly's it will be time for you and I. Heaven if one with God the commandments of life prevailed if failed to hell your soul will sell only in time. In Heaven's line the answers you will find in your mind the last prayer to pray it will be judgment day. As you wait for what God has to say rather allowed in Heaven's gate or the Devil will capture you take your soul away. When it begins either the curse will be broken or the emptiness within will trend as we are possessed by our sins. Which lead to eternal bleeding or forgiven threading the needle in our skin. The line will be formed may be reborn the wings in time once you reach outer heaven will form. Now I will foresight just a sneak peak of God and I close your eyes breathe imagine and believe. After waiting in line finally, it's me the gate open I get lead to God my king I finally see. I kneel before God to honor him I stand up and it all begins. He begins there he sat on a throne but there were angels to condone my judgment for he was not alone. I was nervous thinking how could this be? God thanking me for completing my destiny then he exempts to the book of we. My whole life I see all of my bad deeds he questions me the Skelton's in my closet Déjà vu. Then he allows me to the next step the reason I was created for I see but need the key to that locked door. It appears the key my reward I walk through to explore open the door but I remembered hearing screams of people descending before. I knew what was coming I was confident but for others they may suffer the consequences. Prior to their bad desires being a menace to society a thief a crook and a liar. Now your time will expire the flames will entire in the pit of fire. At this time there are only two ways to go who knows what God will say but every day pray you ascend on judgment.

474. A journey: I'll walk eternity to find my way looking for light a better life a better day. There's so much to do as I pray so much to learn not much to earn. As life plays it turns my bridges I can't burn. My soul yearns for guidance shall I travel the direction of the wind I hate that I've lived my life through sins. It seems the Devil would offend trying to win hoping my life ends demons to this world he has sent. My journey a holds more than I'll ever know. In order to succeed my fears, I have to let go to find answers to my questions is unquestionable. As a man shall I strive to grow I will face deception in the heat, rain, and snow. I know my journey will only be completed when I see a rainbow. It's only me left for humanity has entered Heaven or hell the rest put to death. It seems life has reset and due to God's request salvation, I must collect. A toddler at first which bloomed to a boy, playing with toys smiles life filled with joy. As I got older I grew paranoid, our generation is weak future technology computers, cell phones, androids. Where is hope? If my angels wings are clipped I cannot fly I cannot float. There is no life guards no life jacket no boats. I'm cold without a coat in transition prior to propositions. As I'm a fisher in a sea forever fishing? Praying and wishing something comes on me different. There needs to be a change. Why have I taken the lord in vain? I have experienced so much pain I'm insane walking to release anger. What shall set me free a hanger? All I fear is danger I'm must a stranger worried endangered. Earth without no one but one man. Life without a mistress I can't bear to stand. It seems my angel is in Heaven Earth she hasn't landed, life is sucking me in as quicksand. I'll cut off my hands thread the needle in my skin to cleanse the dirt within. I'll cut out my eyes to see what it's like to be actually blind then only with my heart answers I'll find. Whatever it takes to escape and begin more divine. I go through a journey for eternity a lifetime looking for a special sign!

475. The wishing wale: If magic were real then this dream I'm forever in would feel tangible no longer would reality be concealed. Cursed since birth planted on Earth still I lurk search hope the pain will disperse. For what the world's worth I couldn't tell? But what are my chances on a dime landing tails? Hoping it will all prevail in the wishing wale. I'm stuck in a maze in a puzzle a stage fearing trouble. How can my destiny depend on a chance a coin within the pocket of my pants? Wait is this true, I found this dime on Earth and somehow in my dream, it carried through. I now have a clue but what shall I do? God, I guess I'll turn this over to you I pray and wait then I find a sign footprints in line of mine. How long will this last? How much time will I not be temporarily blind? This must be a hallucination in my mind I still strive and gave it a try. I ended up at the last footprint for in my eyes I could tell I saw it for myself the wishing wale. I approached with caution for I think it's a trap by the Devil and he's watching. I feel God in me so could this dream not sail? I pulled the dime out of my pocket closed my eyes and hope tails doesn't fail. I threw it in and it landed right then right before my eyes I saw the light. Out of spite, the day has ended it is night I see no dark then the voice in the wale spoke and it all starts. The sound waves traveled to my ear I hear fast beating of my heart for my spirit ascended out of my body I was torn apart. All I heard was "you have one wish to be granted in my mind I said to be one with God in Heaven at the end. But on Earth somehow my poetry God will speak through me. Life I will understand the Intel then it happened I saw my whole life flash my legacy to God my soul did sail. I woke up in Outer Heaven visiting the wishing wale.

476. If there's a will there's a way. There comes a time of the day when we hope to reach something so we pray. With God if there's a will there's a way! It's not about what you say actions speak louder than words don't overlook a situation by your nerves because in, a spark of a moment things can curve. The will is your pride hiding inside as you decide to set aside deprive and realize ways to strategize. There's always a way to achieve but you must believe then results you will receive. Do not listen to negativity those who envy you with jealousy. Positivity must be true in what you say and never forget if there's a will there's a way!

477. Dear diary: Dear diary, is this how it's supposed to be? I'm writing to you because the end is near and I hear voices in my ear muttering the Devil will appear my dear. I'm forever blind the full picture is not clear but life in my eyes is all I see. I remember you telling me your secrets are safe with me. Still my eyes bleed of what I see a cold world too blind to see the underworld the secret among society. Humanity a last of dying breed cursed since birth especially one's like me, not a planted seed. But somehow I regard on the deck of cards of succeeding in life and going far. Dear readers of my diary I won't you to please open your eyes and see greed is grief depression is misery our past is our history. Life is a puzzle such a mystery. How can we break the curse upon human beings? When money is the root of all evil. Life's a big competition all God's children but viewed not equally. Must be emissive hard for my mind to be comprehensive, when I'm stuck in a dimension writing a book of we a fisher in a sea forever fishing. I stare at God in the sun he glistens I pray I hope he listens and foresight my visions bringing words of wise to my pride as I decide with precision. I know I got to obtain the key to success with ambition show and tell to the wishing wale for my wish to prevail to understand Jesus Christ see the light and visit the Devil in hell. Hoping I will receive a possibility in life the truth Intel to impel telekinesis to propel. Help the world saved by the bail hoping my messages to a soul would receive in mail only time will tell. Do you see what I see? Do you feel what I feel? I know the Devil is a lie and God is real. But chances are odd to be one with God when the earth is such a steep hill. Selling your soul is a deal or no deal can't you tell? The world is created for us to fail a living hell. To humanity stuck in jail poverty can't afford bail. I swear if God came to this place all the evil he would erase. On Judgement day, we would stand face to face to see the true meaning of grace. When my soul has journeyed out of space my words will never go away. So please those who read remember me to my heart life in my eyes is received. The end of my legacy is planned with you dear diary.

478. I see death around the corner: Living in a hateful world I anticipate ways to reinstate my fate but I fear it's too late. It's hard to let go my fears soon the secret among society will appear I see the end of my demise it's clear. Starring through my rear view here is a clue soon to my love ones they will take me away from you. My eyes bleed and this vision leads shall they succeed will my legacy I achieve? Must be too soon earth is my tomb. Heaven is my sanctuary and to them after this book is published my downfall will be necessary. Still I ascend the stairs I won't give in I swear I see now even in my sleep I accept my fate. I'm in too deep they will attack me as like many Tupac, Biggie, Malcolm X, Martin Luther king. It's the truth we know for we can't show but many will expose enough and trust soon I will be a goner. If torture is deception resurrecting a loner I see death around the corner.

479.   The pride of a black panther: We are a community fighting for justice and freedom from all our protesting look at the world nothing has come. Still no peace on our streets still stuck in jail and poverty the 27 amendments of our constitution results to no irony. But actually, the ten point program we only live to be following. We demand to be treated equal still it's evident we provide our own defense. Now that the world has experienced a black president what does that represents? Change Obama is perusing constantly moving the shadow that forever follows are brotherhood is Huey P Newton. We stand and fight never a coward we represent black power. What does the Black Panther represent pride for our legacy we shall die but let others recognize? It's takes a community in God's hand one nation which it stands. No black man shall expand in the military command. We demand are rights put here to fight So much police brutality so how could we be polite? Indignant of our everyday life can u see fear in our eyes planned to attention not surprise. Spread the black power and feel our pride.

480.   Let go: I Just got to let go some things off my chest. A couple months ago God sent me my first sign. I see the ladder of life now I all I do is climb. But I find it's never-ending then in came this vision. As I write with my pen using precision blessed with a gift to me God's given. Then I was ascending the stairs aware and beware felt pressure beneath my feet. Walking In my sleep with faith too blind to have sight seems obsolete. I got close to the top the hill was too steep then mentally and spiritually my soul was cut deep. I felt weak but uncompleted then a dream took me on a ride I had no choice but to take a seat. Then at the top of the stairs I saw two doors and two keys then in my ear I heard a voice whispering to me he said ''pick the left one it must have been the Devil cause instantly I felt heat. My heart thundered I was traumatized and paralyzed saw death right before my eyes the end of my demise. He crept, winked I blinked. In my mind, I said how could this be? He laugh and said 'finally he got me'' Then God whispered in my ear said ''there's always a way out'' I felt my pen in my pocket then I imagined me carving my way out. I closed my eyes then the door disappeared I walk to the other door still holding my fears then God appeared it was clear. When I glared feeling impaired but nothing to beware. I had a conversation with God it was amazing from the begging but the bad part is it only last 4 minutes. I cried to God and ask why so many to Heaven fly? I felt mourned cause last week my friend died and before that my other friend committed suicide. At that point, I felt alive visit the dark side and reached the other side. Time was ticking it was about to end I reached for God's hand but the dream ended. I haven't forgiven that God blessed me with a gift it's my Destiny. To my true bros please have faith in me. I been gone for a while still I hold a smile because I'm only going to be here for a while. Still feeling stress and I guess I got to watch every calculated step hope to progress and the keys to success I shall collect. Hoping with my words to every soul it connects. Just so you know I had to let go some things off my chest.

481. Poetic justice: Words can heal a soul when air reaches a heart of a broken window. The stars will shine then in mind you will find a moment of time. The right one restores put the pieces together then it's all in line. It can start with dislike but soon the flower will adapt and bloom right. Rather in the day but never in one night the seed grows as the connection based on your selection. When it's real love becomes such a blessing. The hard part is letting out are confessions getting over depression. Stuck among one getting over obsession. When you flush the pain away then hits another recession. Our mind can play tricks on us nearly contraception. All sunshine clears rain in exchange a rainbow and a new love to gain. To obtain the poetic measure is forever just like a flower successfully blooming without water how could you trust it? Love is pain and where is love without justice.

482. Pornography: A temptation a bad image to see women we wrongly perceive in pornography. An addiction affecting all who saw. This is met for none now look what has come? Women flaunting their figures advertising to get bigger but for what is this how it's supposed to be? For stress to flee sex is received for another to another they attend and leave. This is grieve poisoning we as a society it wrongly shapes the brain nothing much to gain. How can those women find the right guy? When all they want is sex to try in the future you'd wonder why? For a guy I know it's the best feeling from fulfilling of appealing. We are actually the villain's this disease still spreads upon humanity affecting us. When I see my eyes bleed viewing pornography.

483. Animals shall be valued like us: Human beings are not perfect but can be amicable. Just like animals these creatures go through enough Animals shall be valued like us. This subject is something I must discuss and trust after ashes to ashes dust to dust. We are reincarnated in the cycle to give nine lives to live. Then we are blessed as an animal a new life by God he gives. Why do people beat wrongly treat our pets? Let's not forget we have to admit it's not adequate. When we miss the big picture not seeing the importance of protection an animal of our selection. Could be a love one through resurrection? These animals have emotions to they do feel affection. They hear words understand as they follow what we command. They are truly our helping hand. So why do we not give love? A hug is never enough. My dear world animals shall be valued like us.

484. A conversation to myself: Who are you? A human being what have you seen? Many dreams times I've fantasized and find stuck in between reality my spirituality working to manage salary. But there's something missing something desperately I need. What is it? Forgiveness, passion, and perhaps a wish. If life were a sea and my dream were bait I have to catch my fish? What do you want out of life? My own family children and mostly a wife someone to commit to love and treat right. Are you sure you are young, not dumb but to the life of ahead partly numb? I am the 1 a child of God he is my father I am his son. I look in my eyes what life has become. The holy fruit an apple a plum either sweet or rotten. You never know what a holds but I ask God for the truth to unfold. What is your destiny? A legacy perhaps whatever God has planned for me. I can't obtain everything things seem strange I'm stuck on a grid an x, y domain. I slightly complain search to restore how to furthermore and gain. Only so long here I shall hang. What is one thing you wish you could do? Go back and sacrifice one thing each sacrifice pays its price a way of life. What is your pleasure a thing you cherish the most? My poetry my words every line which defines times. Adjective pronouns nouns a bad situation a nightmare something lost. As the curb is clear clearance to ride along here I have no fear. I'm watching near my dear, you have written many things prayed many prayers God is inevitable. To learn lessons Earn blessings of turns. What is it you feel you need to do? I need, more of I want I feel that I can rewrite the bible refill the seven sculptures missing. I know the world will treasure it when God talks I must listen. God has given you a sign what do you find a 20 dollar bill 20 for maybe by 20 I will release my book 500 which was on the right corner of the bill I got this sign twice 500 poems in my book 5(0/0/)5+2= 7 sculptures hidden in my book. God, I need your guidance I have questions and need help hopefully things dealt won't melt. From all, I felt a conversation with myself.

485. One with god: I believe once the spirit hidden in us we fully see we've complete our destiny. The light will appear it will come clear it's finally here were one with God. Our souls are no longer broke no longer cold. Now life is gold now behold the words of the wise will be rightfully told. God will stick on you like mold this can happen young maybe old. From the experience of life possessed by our sins. Finally accepting salvation letting God in thread the needle in our skin. It will begin soon to ascend no longer will Devil be a parasite. We can now fight the eternal light will pod when we finally reach one with God.

486. A trip to heaven: It is time, the birds will sing God will call. As Heaven recalls no worries no more sorrows no more pain leading to tomorrow. The grim reaper will appear but do not fear the answers to your outcry ending the end of your demise will come clear. Your peers shed tears you can hear it. Thinking to yourself it this serious? Then in a spark of a moment, you let go death what you are fearing. The angel comes on your spirit to attend reaches out and grabs your hand Heaven soon to blend. Now you must follow to your pride this will be much to swallow the emptiness within will dissolve no longer hollow. A dream for most especially preachers and revenues a trip to Heaven. It will be dark but the light will guide you through. As angels, family, friends, and God awaits for you. You don't see the big picture still you have a clue. You have journeyed out of the world you see Heaven's gate. Stand in line as it is judgment day. You sweat shake and cry asking God so many questions so many whys. You realized you have died but holding your pride God leads you to 2 doors for your destiny and tells you to pick a door and key. Heaven or hell soon to see once rightfully conceived outer heaven will soon be a foresight for you and me. More barring than any moment or memory a trip to Heaven.

487.   War world3: This a nightmare opposite of a dream soon to effect America our entire country war world3. Who knows who it can be between but this fight will last long in the ring? As military man expand are clan must apprehend a win. When it begins a crisis will start cities will be torn apart. The world will be filled with dark this war will be different for the president is the bail like a sausage the allies will hold the president hostage. Shall we give in salute when on our country they threaten to nuke? What will come then? As are luck will run thin the chances to win at that point is odd. The way to overcome this is God as there is always a way out. My eyes bleed of what I see someone close with the planning maybe the secret among society will cause world war 3.

488.   1-10: 1 man started this world created all boys and girls. 2 human beings were a test to humanity Adam and Eve. 3 kings couldn't conquer everything 3 queens as Queen Elizabeth condemned a false team. 4 millennium still hasn't descended to us. It was, at first, a land before time something we couldn't vividly see. 5 million and more now exist ancestors descending it seems reputation hasn't missed. 6 days the Earth, Heaven, and outer world was created. A man before mankind a lifetime, timeline not properly dated. 7 days in a week 700,000 would follow God 10% of that probably would lead to "he" 8 species which furthermore, 8 slaves died before 8 plus many more have followed God. Noah Egyptians Indians a breed before cursed seeds. 9 lives of an ancient cat 41+9 stars represent America 9 stages to mazes a book of life without 7 sculptures perhaps 9 faces. 10 people are equal the other 10 are born. Different 10 lies 10 truth's still something is missing. 10 days of Hell an eternity in jail without God 1-10 would fail.

489. The day you read my soul: To my friends and foes who could ever know how a flower beneath a concrete would grow? The day you read my soul my past u will know. All this pain in my blood in my veins is the reason I remain insane. Living through struggle but I can't complain. One day fame I will obtain but life is such a dirty game. Of my soul, I feel ashamed but my savior, the lord is his name. Inside my mind, I feel blind seeing reality lies. Without eyes the Devil I despise but he is the reason for my outcry. The day u read my soul is when I die. May the angel come for me its destiny shall we fly to heaven up high. To my peers everywhere shedding tears soon it will all come clear. The air I breathe will no longer feel cold my story shall be told. As you read the truth will unload the day you read my soul.

490. Black history: From the 1600's to late 1800's African Americans were in slavery. Segregated regulated perpetrated in my eyes I'm devastated. What happen to so many human beings? For this is black history from Rosa Park, Malcolm x, the black Panthers, Martin Luther king (Jr) and many suffering an epidemic. A nation with justice diminish what did they do to disserve that. For what went all wrong disgrace upon a face of a skin tone. Suffered pain down to the bone many was not alone. They were forced to fight in wars. Suffered segregation got no education couldn't learn to read. Now look at today what African Americans turn out to be. We can accomplish anything are first black president we have received. But still society deceives mischievously which leads to trials and tribulations of one nation with dedication. Still justice holds stipulations I dedicate this to one's like me. Look at the evolution of black history.

491. Adam and Eve: The first human beings creating everything for humanity. Adam and Eve because of thee, we have received animals insects they name them all. In our eyes life begin but they two were possessed by there's sins this was how it begin. God created Adam and eve as a test to resemble us. First it was Adam then of the ribs of Adam he created Eve to have a mate for Adam. There was a tree with poisoning fruit for God didn't want them to eat. The Shepard of the garden deceived eve when she proceeded wrongly. Now God has forever cursed human beings for this recreation leads to us not being perfect. The two honors were to be fruitful and multiply. But I find eating the Apple was wrong this is why the fruit represents a seed and because of grief this distortion represents today as an abortion. As fortune played its part love sparked the two were evidently torn apart. Where was cupid with his dart? To aim among a broken heart. God forgave but we have received a legacy to the blood line of our ancestors, Adam, and Eve.

492. Life will truly be met: The castles held deputies, for if prominence thy king who if descended would be supreme. Through airy region scheme was of slavish soldiers condemned a false team. Peasants quarry between, land of trail frail a lavish trail so thy ring the bell. Where would they sell? Redemption Heaven or convention Hell? It seems history prevails life liberty pursuit's conspiracy. Events strike upon seconds the clock of life has an existence. The world to a naked eye full life, matter, eyes can't reach deceit. Secrets seem to hide imprinted textures of signs read between lines. As the author found the ladder of life then climb. The bible holds substantial proof the youth despise the truth. The elderly or Gods refugees conceived as a troop. Dreams alternated means, what is the real story of God? The ancient myth contradicts if God exist. Sculpture trends salvation hands some don't believe. Some are blind the Devil deceives. Some the light they receive a message they conceive. They say spirituality if one kneels before "he" souls collides. This is the most sensational resolution for you and me. A loss which was brought for a promising cost. Sinning is a fault learn and taught symbolized by devilish thoughts. Every action by God is stalk the tree of life the seed which bloom to a stomp springing out simplicity. Funny how it still found a way to grow despite the dirt the sins buried underneath the leaves. Around the tree is life humanity the weather afflicted upon these leaves which descended to human beings. Time will be complete when the last leaf falls. The sky will fall God will call as the angels recall. To the reality of this, all are small. Wars have brawl evolution seems to crawl. Our lifeline timeline stands tall reality is but a protocol. The ancient pilgrim's statues hidden underneath Egypt the secret hall. As there the truth will evolve. Answers shall dissolve amendments are commandments in God's law. It sums up to religions Christian's and all. A man wrote the bible there are different bibles different beliefs and conspiracies. Where at the end we will reach treasuries are breached. Life is a sea the ocean Heaven, Atlantic the circumference is gigantic. The Intel is frantic waves are souls enjoying the day. Tides abide spirits collide. Who would think we could reach the other side alive? Air is what trees provide. It resides life the sky is our altitudes morally height. The sun is the day the moon is the night. Jesus Christ is our light the Devil promotes eradication to life. Everything is invisible out of sight. Some say actions among spirits and demons are out of spite. At times, our eyes shine brightly our heart ignites our soul excites. Once we become one with God we see the light. When face with death due to survival salvation will be met. Sins are a liability misery is eating our flesh. The truth angels protect. As afterlife, the chosen collect the truth of life will project. There are no ending life resets. As I resurrect away with my flesh I take away no depth. Only if memory is kept life will truly be met.

493. The hidden teleporter: I'm in a dream in Heaven for I have a destiny in outer Heaven. God has hidden a surprise I must figure out why? To obtain I will do more than trying for my purity is not shy. It's not trouble but I must act with patience being subtle. All of sudden I'm back in a path of a maze to connect to the secret chest. I was impressed but eager to explore. I arrived at the door I know which one to open and explore. Right before God speaks to me '' for its unknown to humanity you will soon see here's a list you must complete perfectly in order to find the hidden teleporter a teleporter" I replied why? " soon you will know why but this chance is a one in a lifetime for it will pass by" I then arrived to step one on the list as I predict. As fate reacts I must find the key in the haystack. Last time it was a needle to overcome evil I guess desperately I must find the sequel. Finally, I found it now what must I do? Step two find the right path to choose to gain closer to step three and not lose. There lived an ancient Egyptian monarch statue which represented to me liberty. For step 3 read fulfill the writing but with poetry. It is dark barely light to see I don't need light to write. So I shall be alright in my pants I always have a pen. I took it out imagined light it ignited then it begin. The pieces of the puzzle got put together for what it said on the statue I can't share. Once it was done it opened a door lie there. I walk in to explore for I was at step 4. This was shocking to me I found a way to redefine a lifeline timeline. There were several places to visit it seemed explicit. Whoever created it had much stacked around uncompleted must have been a hoarder. In my eyes, I see the hidden teleporter! I walk close slowly then God spoke to me "Now you see what's ahead of your legacy" I walked in excited to take it for a spin my first stop was in the event of Adam and Eve a beautiful most interesting thing to see. The Garden of Eden was there and the first two human beings compared. I saw the mistake they made the deception of the Shepard he gave. This had me in a daze I was amazed I only had four minutes to explore. Then I found the next stop the Land before time they were Dinosaurs, creatures that are extinct and more. This was amazing I saw a Terex and many other dinosaurs. This was impossible to miss. I thought to myself how could this be? Then I arrived at a new stop it was in the crisis of slavery. For it wasn't a good site to see, how could this be? Man disgraced upon their nationalities no way to escape. I arrived the last place in my mind to be known the Underground Railroad. For no one could see me I was only a shadow. Slaves escaped but only a handful. Then time was up I await for a new place. I was brought in the crisis of the holocaust. There were in Poland with Hitler and his man killing for wrongful reasons. They were having a meeting the teleporter took me to the time of segregation. I saw it the separation among white and black in fact brutality of the police among my people as they attached. I arrived at Martin Luther King (Jr) speech I had a dream then it happened the shot beamed. I closed my eyes still no justice redeemed. I arrived at the bus where Rosa Park refused to give up her seat. As she was seized by the police taken to jail. I knew the world was created for us to fail a living hell. Then to the future, the teleporter prevailed. It was after our time I could tell. There were flying cars ascending far the constitution was different. Politicians, the government, and the president seemed to be missing. Police were looking to bring cause as if they were fishing. The sun was out it glisten then in the spark of a moment the sun disappear. The moon appeared full it was dark. I then prayed to God then it all had started. I ask why me and is this how it's supposed to be?

He replied "My son, you know why it's written in your poetry it's time you come back to me but first take the teleporter where it belongs then I'll send an angel to bring you to Heaven your home back to me" I arrived at my destination with motivation my heart was beating my mind racing. For this was too much for my eyes to see then the angel came for me. I was again let free Heaven soon to arrive. I experience it all until the end of the time. The light was in order before I left my spirit swept. Goodbye, teleporter!

494. The event of God's demise: He must be killed! His astonishing presence is an opposite of a blessing for us. Let's capture and kill him! Seems today misfortune has shine on God and the light got overwhelmed by the dark. For in the event of God's demise starts. He was different from others his purity told him apart. Because of a men with a cold hearts. A loss upon a cross was brought and God was torn apart. When this begin they threaded the needle in his skin opposite of being a friend. Tortured him on a cross so much pain was brought. Every sacrifice pays its price that choice was made right. Which gave every human being eternal life. As it came to end in my dream it caught me by surprise. I cried oh why? He spoke in his mind sending me a sign. Let me free! I cried how could this be? He spoke this is not the end for you and me especially humanity. I knew God wouldn't lie I didn't despise. There in my dream the hidden teleporter lied, the teleporter took me back to my time on a ride. It shocked my pride I witnessed the event of God's demise.

495. Trapped: Stuck in my dream must be a nightmare. I see the Devil right there, God please send me back I feel trapped. Perfection I lack soon I will slip up and he will attack. How must I react? Let go my fears and subtract? In fact, I hear screams of others in my head it must be packed. I see myself sleeping but how do I get out no one hears me when I scream and shout. I know there's always a way out but I must figure out. In my soul I feel cold I walk around with faith as I was told. My hearts beats slowly as if I'm old. I will get out this maze complete this puzzle. I feel trouble so I pray if I shall die before I wake. My soul please God take if destiny has a light then guide me through. God let me find my way for its dark mentally but spiritually I feel torn apart. Then there lies a door but I furthermore with extreme caution. As I reach my hand to open and explore I walk through the door. I know fate isn't a liar and my time has not expired. But am I entire in the pit of fire? What doesn't God want most for the Devil to acquire?. Then a burst of flames exchange for he replies "I know your name your soul is all I want to claim" I replied are you insane! I'm with God on a journey a lane. He replied I'm glad you came there's no way out only water can overrule a flame which you don't obtain but don't worry your purity I'll drain for I'll send you back to God and he'll know you came" I asked him what do you want from me? He said "your gift" my poetry? "yes you are blessed and the words you possessed I cannot let once your legacy is met I won't ever forget for I cannot let'' in my mind I said I bet. ''You have a chance to leave if you can write one poem meaningful enough to intent me Not only will I let you go but one more visit to me is what I owe now it's time to show'' I replied close your eyes I held my pride as I decide to set aside if I can trust him and die. I don't need light to write nor a pin, from the times I've sinned the bleeding of ink in my skin, will lend. A rule I have to bend it happened I wrote it on a wall he saw my flaws the Skelton's and all. He said ''the words were too small'' God then called and react as he turned back his promise he told to visit once more I won't forget that. I escaped woke up in Heaven no longer trapped.

496.   Dear Devil: First Lucifer I'd like to say hello Dear Devil, I know you're waiting for me to sin. I decided to accept salvation threading the needle in my skin saying to myself never again. You are the opposite of a friend every commandment you have bend. Which leads to where you are down below in the pit of fire. For your own reasons along with your demons your gracious empire. But I desire Heaven God requires me to complete my legacy. I know in the past you got the best of me. Still I feel pressure beneath my feet respiratory accepts defeat. I ascend the stairs in my sleep in my dream you I've seen. You try so hard to come between me and God to intervene. I'm with God it feels odd that I'm writing to you. But at the time, I was trapped didn't know what to do. I'll soon come visit you to show you can't win. When it begins the truth will reveal inside how I feel I must let go. For there's so many skeleton's only you and God know. I hide pride it doesn't show I beg for forgiveness and ask God to baptize my soul. Devil, your presence scatters you're just an obstacle. A shadow of dark a man with a frozen heart. Physically, mentally, and spiritually torn apart. I want you to know you can stop this, now that you rot, hell is hot you can fix things with God in Heaven earn a spot. Then the madness will stop the curse will be broken you think I'm joking? I'll give you a key to that closed door the door will open. But this is shameless to your heart you rather skip this moment I know. All this hate you're condoning what is it for? I look in your eyes seeing what's in stored. I know you exempt from pain but want it to stop. Now here's your shot! Surrender or continue to rot. Turn in flames that are forever hot. They can cool down if you act now. Water overrules fire and to entire past your evil desire prior to God's empire. It's your choice, I can remember hearing pain in your voice opposite of rejoice. This is all for you, you're the individual the shadow of dark is your reciprocal. A message for you to know dear Devil.

497.   God and the Devil: After escaping the trap of the Devil I experienced life in my eyes on a new level. I must figure out the journey of God and the Devil. So I prayed before I lay me down to sleep lord send me to Lucifer I must go back for he owes me a visit he speaks ''My son I have fear but I'll let you through'' at the end God please send me back to you. For I need the truth to reveal the answers to carry through. I closed my eyes then my dream took me along. I woke up in the pit of fire the place I don't belong. I walked searching for light of the shadow that follows me reflects because it is dark. That's when Satan appeared then it all starts I see you have come back for what I owe now behold this place is opposite of cold but I feel ok for the spirit hidden in me has pushed the heat away. Satan you must tell me what happened between you and God what intervened? he replied "okay this your lucky day but here you cannot pray he laughed let me think back to the old mighty God ha! This is odd well I didn't want to no longer be an angel living under his rules so I took fate into a duel the flames I forever obtain is the fuel now me and my demons are cruel" for in my eyes they all appeared but I didn't fear "I couldn't take it anymore why should I furthermore to find the key to that closed door Why should I be let free and soar Instead I am God enemy what I feel is why misfortune has shined on me now I have received my own legacy I hate humanity" I see his pain now but I couldn't feel his misery feel his pain at that point things weren't the same" how could this be fixed I said "there's no fixing the past God's immortal and I'm dead instead of eternal life seeing the light which is how it starts I'm forever in the shadow of dark torn apart without a heart staying down no need to smile you see I'm used to it! Now I couldn't have to react the cards have stacked the answers unpacked God send me back! I appeared in outer Heaven "My God is this true? "most of it is overdue Satan was the Shepard that deceived Adam and Eve it's why we are possessed by our sins which spread a curse upon humanity that's why to hell he is received eternally" my eyes bleed now you see there is a dark side reached clearance an evil spirit this was in my eyes unrevealed on a different level the story of the God and the Devil.

498. A-Z: A: All for one, ascend the stairs always believe in God. B: break fee be who you are and supposed to be. If you believe you can achieve blessings will be brought. C: Can't is no such thing collect the key to success complete our legacy's. There is a spot in Heaven for you and me. D: Direct respect shall be kept collect the key to the secret treasure chest. Don't take the lord in vain. Day of the dead don't judge a book by its cover. Don't think God isn't undercover. E: Every day we shall pray if I shall die before I wake entering Heaven's gate. Everyone deserves a second chance everyone needs to believe in God faithfully. Far away is where we shall stay for us to never give up we must pray. When times are rough free you and me out of poverty. Prejudice disgrace upon race a face which was placed from God. G: God is love the spirit of God is more than a kiss or hug more addicting than a drug. Glance at the world in my eyes give your all or nothing. Give what you want out of life God is everything. H: Hello world boys and girls. High above is our world hope is the key for "he" is with you and me. Hell is hot not a good spot. I: If I shall die before I wake I pray I earn a key to Heaven's gate. I'm the same as you but to life have many clues. I love God and hope you do to.

I wrote this book for all of you I'm only me building a legacy striving to be free. Desperately I will leave I love you all have faith in me. I write what I feel imagine and see. J: Just believe and everything will work out for you. Jokes don't promote hope when we are tied against the rope. K: Kiontae Pettis is my name for the world will know I came. Keep your head up in God we must trust. Killing is not the answer kites can't reach Heaven. L: Let the sunshine clear the rain love yourself but morally God. Listen to learn blessings you shall earn. Look into a mind search to find life is what you make it. Levels of life contain the Devil. M: money is the root of all evil. Money can't buy you happiness many people die many people sin for reasons I don't know why. Minutes defines time. N: never say never, never give up, not is giving up a chance to a shot. A Nests is in Heaven where we shall rest. O: over the rainbow is where I shall go. On the road if it's a journey, over is soon to come off track come back over react. Bad results may come back oven is heat representing "he" P: pornography hurting the brain of you and me. Presents past will forever last please forgive me. Lord pressure is always close perfection is competition a deadly obsession. Q: quest as life is a test and resembles a treasure chest. R: respect all remember me rain will wash away the pain resolution of our constitution because life is an illusion. Ready to stand before God resembles that life assembles rise above madness. S: Soulmate from fate I hope God has created one for all she, we shall appreciate. Spreading all around sex super and beyond. Support the poor success shall be met. Separate the evil sinning is not winning solving problems take time. Selections continuing depression the end of time there's no such thing as perfection take time on what's yours and mine. Under is not for us undefined because reality hides. V: visualize my words versatility is watching our mobility. Valentines can be hard to find variation is our nation the vaccine is to break this curse which shall one day reimburse. W: when will it rest? We are all equal no one's the best. When will there be peace on our streets? Why do we not extol God? World war 3 will start. X: x-mas is the birth of Jesus Christ. Xenophobia is within the media xerography looks like the future to me the best book to read. Y: you can be what God sent you to be yes Heaven is created for human beings yours truly. Z: zeal to God shall I kneel this is life in my eyes for you and me a through z!

499. Eucharist: God and his disciples 12 apostles had a special prayer to pray. In the event of this God demise sacrificing his son Jesus Christ humanity has been relief of sins. As God son punished upon a cross a lost which eternal life was brought. In means Before Jesus ascended for those in who witness his evolution before our world descended. God and his disciples with last supper to celebrate although due to eternity there clock of existence wouldn't regulate. So they had a special prayer to pray not for humanity but for the truth that religions can hide the real belief. Therefore it will be "he" to wrongly deceive those who don't see that no matter what means deception hides in refuges falsely condemning. Evolution resides a solution for those are blind and numb relying on a false philosophy. For Earth is hell for humanity not morally living but based upon decisions there will be not much purity given. Laws of nature, nature of cause as the truth dissolves. For there is always a cause as the world evolves. How many can pray for something more important than what a mind gathers? For some rather believe but not receive the complete back story upon their beliefs which can deceive. In God's home the air to his throne for dinner is served and before we value the holy food which we consume may we resume to a prayer which abide. Those to be divine in a spiritual cocoon for those who are blind and cannot find the way out of their mind judgment day would be their tomb. Non-acceptance of fate would be their doom. The first prayer for him as God created life the second prayer for the church of christ and last for the supper of his disciples around the table. On Earth it would be enable but a demon demand upon sins would disable. For those at the supper had a halo-receiving the light in eucharist.

500.   This is the end: Prior to my desires all, I require as a way to God's empire. The sinning and fire I now retire. Wash away my sins throw me in the dryer. Shall I rise way higher? Hoping time with God will never expire? Life's a dream fake reality a fatal scheme as shall my spirituality stay clean. Let none intervene the words that are flowing I really mean. Lord find me break my closed door I need eternal Christ. What are you waiting for? I'm ready to give in let it begin threading the needle in my skin. Then I shall pray every day somehow I must find a way to survive through another day. I look at people and find lost souls lost minds losing time committing crimes. Which resign to climb leave it behind doing a little better than hits pressure. Temporarily but on others lasting forever. Shall we be cursed looking for a cure? There's no magic it's tragic I look past it. Seeing others life style poor others lavish. We want but don't have it. Shall we beg for forgiveness hope God's grace upon every race? Replenish get a new blessing this is the end my last call my message. There the ending to my blessings of my poetry. All though there is no way out of poverty causing depressing. Using weapons mind aggression I have millions of confessions. Many obsessions this forever no recession. Even though many are stressing when the end is near my legacy shall still be here. What you believe in can come true. Your spirit is coherent I'm still near. For I will in the end disappear life's not fair. When I sit and stare I then compare what's not fair. Praying others will take care I don't do this just for me but believe all those that do read will hope to achieve. Let out greed but succeed through my poetry to lead a growing seed. Soon to grow and let others know how to God thou shall never let go. For the rose underneath the concrete will show. Just so you know the world is losing control. A broken heart nearly torn apart from the start. So many dead in prison on probation or parole. For God, they don't extol which flowed to a bumpy road. A steep hill the Devil possessing many to kill. Nothing but rage filled a trill deal a wrongly curse spread leading to a plague spilled.

But hiding inside to show no appeal concealed not even pain pills can stop the pain. Let the sunshine wash away the rain a needless gain. Others are insane taking the lord in vain too many cars broken too many lanes. Lots are chasing fame to obtain but competition leading to a dirty game. Shall God appear rain show he has come? Wipe away this Earth let ones with thirst in Christ in Heaven's gate first reimburse? Though God gave his word to never to Destroy again this will be the end no stopping. This deadly apocalypse only time to pray not to slit your wrist shed a tear of fear. The end is near ball your fist this is my last wish. God I ask to be brought back to thug's mansion live my life in expansion. Born in the ghetto-trapped in a spider of a black Weddle. Let us assemble to a new level Christ will tremble. Out with the Devil though I know soon I will die. Maybe killed or it will come by surprise? Every day wondering why? Shall my soul fly like you and me to all let God furthermore to an open door an eternal reward? What we were placed in this world for to not fry. A message and the end for you and I my fellow family and friend's goodbye this is the end!